Per Barbara & K.C. MURPHY
Grazie mille
Mollie

Trattoria Mollie's

Primi Piatti

First Course

By Mollie Ahlstrand

Photography by Tessa Matyas

Trattoria Mollie's
Primi Piatti, First Course

Editor/Producer: Ali Ahlstrand
Food and cover photography: Tessa Matyas
Designer: Jackie Goodman

ISBN: 978-1-4522-8267-1

CONTENTS

continues

Introduction

*W*ould it surprise you to learn that you can put three beautiful Italian courses on the table in less than half an hour? Contrary to what's often thought, Italian food—that is, food as the Italians really cook it—is very easy to make. The key is fresh, high-quality ingredients; with those on hand you need only a few simple techniques to serve a lovely and memorable meal.

What drew me to the Italian way of eating in the first place (besides the fact that is it delicious, of course!) is the casual way it's prepared and offered to friends and family. In Italy, all guests are like family. "Come on in! Don't even call!" Food is served with love and warmth. Italian food is also surprisingly healthy, and that includes pasta. I myself eat pasta yet I've managed to stay thin all these years because I eat it as the Italians do—as an appetizer accompanied by a small portion of fish or chicken with some vegetables on the side.

I would like to see Americans avoid canned and frozen convenience food. Not only are most convenience foods processed with lots of unhealthy fats, sugar, salt and additives, they deprive you of the pure flavor of fresh food. Plus, there really is no need to eat all these highly processed and fried foods. I know that everyone is pressed for time these days, but many authentic Italian dishes can be placed on the table in 20 to 30 minutes. Talk about fast food! Italian cooking, when prepared as it is by Italians, proves that even the busiest person needn't rely on mediocre-tasting foods with unhealthy

ingredients. The simple, fresh and light dishes on these pages are the same ones I've been serving for 17 years at my restaurant, Trattoria Mollie, in Montecito, California.

It's not every day that you find an Ethiopian woman running an Italian restaurant in a West Coast beach town, but I have always felt at home in this beautiful place, which is not unlike coastal Italy in both attitude and altitude. I was actually born and raised in Mekele, a small town in northern Ethiopia that Italy once attempted to occupy and later had many Italian immigrants. My father spoke the language because he worked with Italians when he was young. So, while Ethiopian and Italian culture might seem far apart, it's not unusual for northern Ethiopians like me to have an interest in all things Italian—and especially Italian food (clothes and shoes, too!).

Montecito, which lies right next to Santa Barbara, is a picturesque Mediterranean-style town with the temperate climate and the laid-back atmosphere that seems indigenous to charming, hilly places overlooking the ocean. As in Italy, there is an appreciation here for what the earth has to offer, extending from the gardens and window boxes all over town to the local bounty of fruits and vegetables fresh from nearby farms.

Santa Barbara has several wonderful farmers markets and one of them is held every Friday right in front of Trattoria Mollie. This gathering of local farmers is right in line with how Italians like to shop. People come to take in the gorgeous sight of greens stacked high on tables, baskets full of tangerines and peaches, and fresh-caught fish sold out of ice chests. They walk the aisles, chat with the vendors and, of course, fill their baskets and canvas bags with food so flavorful that it needs little enhancement. You can leave the market with a few tomatoes, a scattering of herbs, some lettuce, lemons, and a piece of snapper, and have all you need for a quick-prep dinner that same night.

One reason I believe Trattoria Mollie has become a favorite with many Santa Barbara customers, including famous locals, is that the authentic Italian food I serve fits right in with the light and healthy way Californians like to eat. Yet food has to be more than healthful to keep customers coming back; it has to taste good and authentic Italian food does because it's made with the best possible ingredients. If you use high-quality ingredients, food really needs little embellishment or fancy cooking techniques to enhance its flavor. And by high-quality ingredients, I don't necessarily mean high-cost ingredients. When you make Italian food in the simple, classic way, it's moderate to downright cheap in cost.

The beauty of this food is that it also tastes so fresh and bright. The flavors are profound, but not overpowering—and Italian cooks like to keep them that way. Please do not ask for A-1 Sauce, Ranch or Thousand Island dressing at an Italian restaurant. It's a major *faux pas*!

Although many people think of Italian food as twenty variations on pasta, Italians rarely make an entire meal out of noodles. Instead, the Italian diet is a well-rounded mix of protein—often fish—served with vegetables and preceded by a small serving of pasta and vegetable-based antipasto. Italians also walk a great deal, traveling on foot to the market, out to restaurants, everywhere!

This life of moderate eating and physical activity is on par with what health experts often write about and try to live by. Everything in modest portions. When you eat this way, you can consume several courses and still end up with a very satisfying but not overindulgent meal. Eat this way and you never have to count calories or feel deprived. And the rewards are many: healthy heart, beautiful skin, and energy for all that life has to offer.

To me, good eating has always been about sitting down at the table to a delicious meal and sharing conversation about daily life. Food helps us connect with the ones we love, but you don't have to spend hours in the kitchen to present a meal that makes your loved ones feel nurtured and appreciated. *Primi Piatti, First Course* is my effort to share the back-to-basics beauty of straightforward cooking. Food that's fresh, quick, and delightful is an Italian tradition.

From Mekele to Montecito

$\mathcal{I}$ am not a big woman. I'm actually only 5-feet tall, but that has never stopped me from taking on a big adventure. I'm a lot tougher than I look! I don't give up on anything. When I'm passionate about something, nothing can hold me down. And one thing I have always been passionate about is learning. I could have stayed in Mekele, the little Ethiopian town where I was born, and lived a conventional life, but I hungered for more. I wanted to see what life was like outside the confines of my small hometown.

My five brothers, three sisters and I had the good fortune to be raised by restrictive, but open-minded parents. My father, a successful businessman, believed that his daughters should be well educated, even though we were a Muslim family and lived in a culture that didn't believe in women's autonomy. His ideas didn't go over very well at the mosque and he was censured for his forward thinking.

My father was also traditional in many ways and there was a lot of pressure on him to make his children conform to Muslim standards. When I was 14, my parents arranged for me to marry a man twice my age. I had already passed the age—13—when it was considered appropriate for a Muslim girl to become a wife. I was removed from school and forced to stay home with my mother, where I became sad and lonely. Finally, I consented to marry and my parents found the older man who consented to be my husband.

At this point, though, some thought I was difficult and some gossiped about me and criticized my headstrong ways. They didn't believe I was a virgin, though they were proved wrong. If I didn't prove that I was virgin my husband and father were permitted to beat me.

The marriage was a disaster and I begged my father to allow me to divorce my husband. It wasn't easy to secure a divorce (I had threatened that if I didn't get the divorce I would convert to Christianity), but we proceeded with the lengthy process. While I was standing before a 50-year-old judge arguing my case, the judge asked my father to approach the bench. Quietly, he told my father that he would be willing to take me as his fifth wife! Thankfully, my father declined. The divorce was granted.

I was anxious to get out of Mekele, but the law required that I wait three months to assure that I wasn't pregnant. Well, I was pregnant so, despite my desire to leave, I needed to stay home. At only 15 years of age, I had no idea the love I later would feel for my son or the gratitude I'd have for his presence in my life. Still, I wanted to make a better life—for both of us.

When my son Ali was still an infant, I left him with my parents and moved to Addis Ababa, the capital city of Ethiopia, to go to school. My brother had moved there after attending a university in Saratoga, New York. He escorted me to and from school and wouldn't let me out of his sight. Again, I rebelled by running away. Only when my father promised to set up a business for me in Addis Ababa, was I persuaded to go back.

I opened a camera shop and began living a very Western style of life, wearing lipstick, driving a car—it seemed I was the first Muslim woman in my town to do so. In the meantime, I also became enchanted with my son. Now older and wiser, I felt joy in motherhood for the first time.

One day an American man by the name of Rex Fleming came into my shop to buy film. He was on the faculty of the Brooks Institute of Photography in Santa Barbara and had come to town to film a commercial for Ethiopian Airlines. By now Ali was living with me and I was concerned about a deformity in his hip. I was longing to leave the country to get him better healthcare and Rex Fleming answered my prayers. He offered to help me get a one-year scholarship to Brooks. I

had to bribe everybody in sight to get out of the country, but I didn't hesitate. I was 26 and on my way to America. Not with my son, though. The Communist regime prohibited me from taking my son out of the country (I couldn't take any money either). It would take another year of hard work before I could find a way to bring him to the States.

I didn't become a photographer after all. Brooks was very hard for me and I eventually dropped out. I continued renting a small room and got a job, still hoping to bring my son to Santa Barbara. One day, I told a friend of mine that I was worried about my son in Ethiopia with bad hip. I was devastated leaving him there but I still didn't have the money to bring him to the United States. "Mollie," my friend told me, "there is a hospital in Los Angeles called Shriners Hospital for Children. They treat children with bone deformities at no charge and sponsor them to come to the country."

It took months of hassling with the Ethiopian government, but I got Ali out of Ethiopia and admitted to Shriners Hospital. I am still eternally grateful to this wonderful group.

So here we were, Ali and me; Ethiopians in a southern California paradise. I was working in a Hallmark card shop when an accountant named Robert Ahlstrand walked in.

After a long courtship Bob and I were married. I was still dedicated to my studies. After Brooks, I enrolled in the University of California, Santa Barbara where I majored in political science. While at UCSB, I decided that I really wanted to study Italian cooking, so my husband and I took a trip to Rome. I didn't go with the intention of making a big change in my life, but once we got to Italy I had an epiphany: I didn't just want to take a cooking class or two. I wanted to stay for the duration that it took to learn to be a professional cook.

I discussed it with my husband and he was entirely supportive. We decided I would stay and he would return to the States. For the next several years I undertook culinary training, apprenticing to chefs in Rome, Umbria and Bologna. Bob visited regularly. It wasn't easy. At times I was lonely. Often I was frustrated. Almost always I was exhausted. But the learning experience was so exhilarating. One of the chefs I apprenticed under (Vissani, in Umbria) was ranked number one in a field of 26,000 Italian chefs. In Rome, at Arturo's Ristorante, the chef taught me how to make incredible pasta dishes.

I was far from home but I had also found my other home: cooking. Italian cooking came as naturally to me as breathing. When I returned to the States I did some consulting and chef training in Seattle, until finally, I created a place of my own. Trattoria Mollie opened in 1992 in Santa Barbara and, two years later, I moved it to Montecito, a small nearby community.

This is where you can now find me just about every day, fussing over the day's delivery of basil and greeting my customers as they come in the door. I love to cook for them. They are such loyal people and so appreciative of good food. Seeing the joy on my customers' faces when they eat healthy, wholesome, flavorful food has made me want to reach out and tell others my secret—though it really is no secret. These cooking basics have been around for generations, but in this age of overbooked schedules, they've somehow gotten lost in the shuffle. *Primi Piatti* is a reminder of how quick, easy—and good for you—authentic Italian food can be.

The Italian Kitchen

There is Italian food in Italy and Italian food here in America. Why do the two often taste so different? It's the technique, plain and simple. With both in mind you'll make dishes that taste like a meal you'd get in a little Tuscan town. In general, Italian food is very, very easy to make. If you can boil water, chop onions and sauté garlic, you're pretty much primed for Italian cooking. There's no reason to be nervous about any of the recipes in this book.

Io mangio cosi, e lei?

"Io mangio cosi, e lei?" means, "I eat like this, how about you?" Before I talk about what you'll need in your kitchen to cook from this book, I want to say a few more words about why I believe the type of Italian food I serve at Trattoria Mollie is so healthy. There are, of course, many studies showing that the Mediterranean diet helps protect against cancer, heart disease and other deadly conditions. But on a more personal level, I have found that a diet built largely on chicken and fish (I don't eat red meat anymore, but believe it's fine in moderation), some pasta and plenty of vegetables gives me tremendous energy and vitality. It helps my skin look

vibrant and keeps me out of the doctor's office, too. Italian food is so delicious, but of course like anything else, it must be eaten moderately. I start my day with some fruit, maybe some cereal, and a cappuccino. I eat pasta for lunch every day. I love my bread, and on occasion I will eat bruschetta or crostini or one of the other bread-based antipasti included in this book. But the yeast in bread makes me feel bloated. My superstition is that the yeast is still rising! That's why I prefer pasta as a starch. I must have my pasta! But it's a small portion—about half the size you get as an entrée in most restaurants, and an accompaniment to chicken or fish. I also eat plenty of vegetables, particularly Swiss chard, broccoli and cauliflower. Simply sautéed in olive oil, they keep the system running regularly and so much better than when you eat a lot of meat. Think about it: Vegetables go easily down the garbage disposal; steak doesn't really go down at all. It's the same in our system.

The basic fact is, what you eat determines how your body works. It affects your hair, your skin and every process in your body. If you eat fresh, good-quality food your body functions

differently: you sleep well, your fingernails grow fast, and your hair and skin look healthy. If you want true beauty, don't spend your money on expensive creams and lotions; spend it on fresh food!

My husband of 28 years, Robert, is American and he used to like the popular foods. Hot dogs. Chips. Popcorn. Sodas, etc. All these foods were beginning to take a toll on him and he gained quite a bit of weight. "People come to my restaurant and pay me for this healthy food!" I'd say to him. "I know," he'd complain, "but I grew up with these foods." Finally, I said, "I'm going to feed you seven days a week and you're going to stop eating all that processed food. In my culture, sodas are for kids!" I made good on my promise and Robert lost 53 pounds in six months! And he has kept it off.

Italian Essentials

Unless I specify otherwise, you can take it for granted that every ingredient called for in this book should be fresh. Try not to take shortcuts. Using fresh ingredients may mean that you have to stop at the market more often than usual. But, more likely, if you plan ahead, you can shop on the weekends and still have fresh food every night. If, for instance, you visit your local farmers market, or go to the grocery store on Saturday, you can buy a week's worth of vegetables and have them at your fingertips as you cook throughout the week (look at my tip on how to store veggies on page 29.)

Before I get to specific ingredients, here are a couple of general ideas about Italian cooking to bear in mind.

- Italian food is best cooked with Italian ingredients. Of those ingredients that you won't be buying fresh (such as pasta, olive oil and so on), I recommend buying as many Italian imports as possible.

- Garlic is an integral part of Italian cooking, yes, but don't overpower your food with garlic—or, for that matter, with cheese. Either one will drown out the flavor of other fresh ingredients. Stick to the amount called for in these recipes. Yes, garlic is good for you; don't overdo it!

- Don't contemplate mixing cheese and fish. Spaghetti with seafood? Fish soup? Don't sprinkle any Parmesan cheese on top. In Italy, it's the law!

Here is all you need to know about Italian food: Eat well. Eat fresh. Eat organic. Eat moderately. Balance it all.

Herbs

Dried herbs are handy, but they alter the flavor of a dish considerably. Anytime I call for herbs in this book, I mean fresh. Don't substitute dried. If you don't have the herbs on hand, leave them out. Better yet, have herbs growing in your yard or in a window box so that you always have them when you need them. Italians generally grow their own herbs (and tomatoes), and I recommend following their example. Something else to keep in mind about herbs is that they don't all mix well. Sage and basil, for instance, don't go well together because both are strong. When you pair herbs, choose one mild one and one strong one; that way, your dish will have a fresher, cleaner flavor.

Tomatoes

Although they are often called for in Italian recipes, I am not a fan of Roma tomatoes. They have no taste! Tomatoes right off your own vines (or those of a local farmer) are best in summer, but since they're not always available, all the recipes in this book call for red cluster tomatoes. These tomatoes are generally hydroponically grown; however, they have good flavor and body. Look for tomatoes that are deep red and firm with the stems attached to the vine. Leave them on your counter to soften slightly. Never put tomatoes in the refrigerator, which turns them mealy and tasteless.

If you must use canned tomatoes on occasion, buy the best quality you can find and then cook them with sautéed onion, celery, carrot and a little salt, to take away the metallic taste the tin leaves behind.

Extra-Virgin Olive Oil

Olive oil can get expensive, but I suggest that you not skimp on this very important ingredient. You don't have to buy the most costly one out there, but choose a good Italian extra-virgin olive oil in the middle price range. The quality of the food you make is directly related to the quality of the oil you use; your food simply won't taste as good if you use a cheap olive oil. Some people recommend buying two types of olive oil: a less expensive one for cooking and a higher-quality one for putting on the table. That is not my recommendation. At Trattoria Mollie, I cook with the same fragrant and well-rounded olive oil I put on guests' tables.

Always choose extra-virgin olive oil that has been cold pressed. This means that the oil comes from the first pressing of the olives and is of the highest quality. It also means that the oil is removed only through physical means, not through the use of chemicals. Olive oils vary in flavor, from strong to mellow. For the dishes in this book, I recommend using an oil that is somewhere in between.

Store olive oil in a cool dark place (but not in the refrigerator) so that it doesn't turn sour. Chances are you'll use it before it goes bad, but to be on the safe side, store it properly.

Parmesan Cheese

There's only one kind of Parmesan cheese I recommend using: Parmigiano Reggiano from Italy. Most markets and cheese shops mark the cheese's name on the wrapping. Authentic Parmesan is golden-yellow in color. For the freshest flavor, buy it in hunks and grate the cheese yourself.

Pasta

Again, when it comes to dried pasta I recommend buying an Italian brand. At Trattoria Mollie I use DeCecco brand, which is available in most supermarkets and comes in all different shapes. Always add a generous pinch of salt to pasta cooking water and never rinse pasta in water after you cook it. You want starch to cling to the noodle; it helps the sauce stick to the pasta.

Ground White Pepper

You'll see that many of my recipes call for ground white pepper. While I like black pepper in certain dishes, white pepper has a subtler flavor.

Storing Vegetables

Wash and thoroughly dry all vegetables, then place them whole—not cut up—in zippered plastic bags. If it's lettuce, wrap it in paper towels before putting it into the bag. Store in the refrigerator; your vegetables should last about one week. Remember, tomatoes should never be put in the refrigerator, but instead stored at room temperature. This goes for cut tomatoes, too. If you only use part of a tomato, wrap it in plastic and leave it on the counter. Use by the next day.

ANTIPASTI
Appetizer

Insalata di Carciofi

Artichoke Heart Salad

If you have the time to make fresh artichoke hearts, great. If not, frozen or bottled ones do just as nicely

- 2 tablespoons extra-virgin olive oil
- 1 clove garlic, chopped
- 2 shallots, chopped
- 2 tablespoons brandy
- 3 cups artichokes hearts
- ½ cup cherry tomatoes, halved

- 2 tablespoons sliced Kalamata olives
- Salt
- Ground white pepper
- 1 tablespoon oregano, chopped
- 2 tablespoons chopped Italian parsley
- 8 slices shaved Parmesan cheese

In a large saucepan, heat the olive oil over medium-high heat. Add the garlic and shallots and sauté until golden. Add the brandy and sauté for 2 minutes or more.

Add the artichoke hearts, cherry tomatoes, olives, salt and pepper and bring to a simmer. Cook for 5 minutes.

Sprinkle with oregano and parsley. Garnish with the Parmesan cheese and serve. Serves 8.

Optional: add grilled chicken.

Insalata Rucola
e Radicchio

Arugula and Radicchio Salad

Arugula and radicchio used to be rarities in the United States. Now, thankfully, you can find them everywhere. Both types of lettuce really make a simple salad so much more interesting.

- 40 ounces baby arugula
- 5 ounces radicchio
- 2 red cluster tomatoes, chopped
- 16 slices shaved Parmesan cheese

Dressing
- 3 tablespoons extra-virgin olive oil
- 2 lemons
- Salt, to taste
- Ground black pepper, to taste

Wash both lettuces thoroughly and dry well. Julienne the radicchio. Set aside. Squeeze the lemons into a small bowl. Whisk in the olive oil, salt and pepper.

Place the lettuces and tomatoes in a large salad bowl. Gently toss with the dressing. Garnish with the Parmesan cheese and serve. Serves 8.

LA CAPRESE

＊─◎─＊

Tomato, Mozzarella and Basil Salad

I find buffalo mozzarella, which I call for here, superior to regular fresh mozzarella. Like the name implies, it's made from buffalo milk (usually a combination of buffalo's and cow's milk). At one time in Italy, mozzarella was only made from buffalo milk. If you prefer, you can use regular fresh mozzarella, but don't use regular mozzarella, which is more elastic and not as delicately flavored as fresh.

- 12 red cluster tomatoes, sliced
- Salt
- Ground black pepper

- 4 balls fresh buffalo mozzarella, cut in half
- Handful basil, julienned
- 3 tablespoons extra-virgin olive oil

Place the tomatoes on a large serving platter. Season with salt and pepper.

Top the tomatoes with the mozzarella halves. Sprinkle with the basil, then drizzle with the olive oil.
Serve promptly. Serves 8.

INSALATA CESARE

❦

Caesar Salad

I'm not sure why Caesar salad is a staple in Italian restaurants—it was invented in Tijuana. Nonetheless, it's Italian in spirit! This version has a creamy Caesar dressing.

- 4 hearts romaine lettuce

Croutons
- 1 loaf Ciabatta bread
- 2 tablespoons extra-virgin olive oil
- 1 clove garlic, chopped
- 1 tablespoon chopped Italian parsley
- Salt, Ground black pepper

Dressing
- 2 anchovies
- 2 cloves garlic, chopped
- 1 tablespoon capers
- 4 tablespoons extra-virgin olive oil
- 1 egg yolk*
- 4 tablespoons heavy cream

- Juice of 2 lemons
- ½ cup mayonnaise
- ¼ cup grated Parmesan cheese, plus more for finishing
- Salt, Ground black pepper

Preheat the oven to 350 degrees F.

Wash the romaine hearts thoroughly and dry well. Chop into bite-size pieces; set aside.

To make the croutons, cut the bread into 1/2-inch cubes and place them on baking sheet. Toss the cubes with the garlic, parsley, salt and pepper. Bake in the oven until golden and crispy, about 12 to 15 minutes. Let the croutons cool.

To make the dressing: In a food processor, puree the anchovies, garlic and capers. When smooth transfer to a large bowl. Slowly add the olive oil, stirring constantly; repeat this process with the egg yolk, cream, lemon juice and mayonnaise, manufacturing cream. Add the Parmesan and season with salt, pepper.

Add the lettuce to the bowl with the dressing and gently toss dressing. Garnish with croutons and, if desired, a sprinkling of Parmesan. Serve promptly. Serves 8.

*If you're uncomfortable using raw eggs, simply omit the yolk.

INSALATA
DI CAMPAGNA

Country Salad

You can't go wrong with this simple salad. To turn it into a full meal, just add chicken strips.

Lettuce
- 2 heads butter lettuce
- 2 red cluster tomatoes, diced
- 1 small onion, diced

Dressing
- 2 tablespoons lemon juice
- 4 tablespoons extra-virgin olive oil
- Salt
- Ground black pepper

Wash butter lettuce thoroughly and dry well. Chop into bite-size pieces and place in a salad bowl. Add the tomatoes and onion.

To make the dressing: Squeeze the lemons into a small bowl.

Whisk in the olive oil, salt and pepper. Gently toss with the salad. Serve promptly. Serves 8.

Insalata di
Funghi e Sedano

⊶⟐⟐⊷

Mushroom and Celery Salad

If the mushrooms you're buying don't already come pre-packaged, choose the smallest ones you can find.

- 20 ounces small mushrooms
- 20 ounces baby arugula
- 1 head of celery, stalks thinly sliced
- 2 red cluster tomatoes, chopped
- 2 tablespoons chopped Italian parsley

- 3 tablespoons extra-virgin olive oil
- 2 lemons
- Salt
- Ground black pepper
- 16 slices shaved Parmesan cheese

Wipe the dust off mushrooms with a wet towel, then slice them thinly. Wash the arugula thoroughly and dry well.

In a large salad bowl, add mushrooms, celery, tomatoes and parsley. Squeeze the lemons over the bowl, then add the olive oil, salt and pepper. Gently toss, add the arugula, then toss again. Garnish with the Parmesan cheese and serve. Serves 8.

Coste e Bietole

―――

Swiss Chard in Tomato Sauce

The stems of chard take longer to cook than the leaves so its best to separate them and add the stems to the pot first. To remove the stem, run a sharp knife along its edges.

- 1 ½ pounds Swiss chard
- 1 tablespoon + ¼ teaspoon salt
- 1 tablespoon extra-virgin olive oil
- ½ cup chopped onion

- ⅓ cup chopped shallots
- 2 cloves garlic, finely chopped
- ½ teaspoon crushed chili flakes
- 1 cup tomato sauce (see recipe, page 74)

In a large pot, bring 3 quarts water to a boil. Separate the chard leaves from their stems. Roughly chop both the leaves and the stems; set aside.

When water reaches a boil, add 1 tablespoon of salt. Add the stems; cover and cook 3 minutes (begin timing as soon as stems are added). Add the leaves; cover and cook 5 minutes more. Drain chard in a colander, then rinse under cold water until

cool. Drain again, squeezing to remove any excess liquid. Chop coarsely.

In a large skillet, heat olive oil over medium high-heat. Add onion, shallots and garlic. Cook, stirring, until golden, about 2 minutes. Stir in red pepper flakes. Add chard and tomato sauce, reduce heat to medium and cook 5 minutes. Stir in ¼ tsp salt. Serve promptly. Serves 8.

Carpaccio con Parmigiano Reggiano

---✦═◎═✦---

Carpaccio with Parmesan Cheese

When you're eating meat raw, you want to make certain that you buy the best quality beef.

- 1 pound raw New York steak
- 6 tablespoons extra-virgin olive oil
- 3 medium lemons, 1 cut into wedges
- Salt

- Ground black pepper
- 2 tablespoons chopped Italian parsley
- 16 slices shaved Parmesan cheese

Slice the steak as thinly as possible (this is much easier if the steak is partially frozen). Place the slices between two sheets of plastic wrap, and pound them paper-thin.

Place the slices on a serving plate and drizzle with olive oil. Squeeze 2 of the lemons over the Carpaccio, then lightly season with salt and black pepper. Sprinkle with parsley and top with the shaved Parmesan. Garnish with lemon wedges. Serves 8.

PROSCIUTTO
E MELONE

⊶≡⊝≡⊷

Prosciutto with Melon

This is so straightforward, you don't really even need a recipe for it. But I thought I'd include it just in case.

- 24 thinly sliced slices prosciutto
- 1 ripe cantaloupe
- 1 tablespoon chopped Italian parsley

Peel and slice the cantaloupe into 8 slices. Drape the prosciutto evenly on a serving plate. Arrange the melon slices on top. Garnish with parsley. Serve promptly. Serves 8.

MEDAGLIONE
DI MELANZANA

✦═══╾

Eggplant Medallions with Pesto

I prefer to use speck (smoked prosciutto) in this recipe—it gives the dish a hint of smoke. Regular prosciutto (or no prosciutto for vegetarians) is fine, too.

Pesto sauce
- 1 clove garlic
- 1 cup basil leaves
- Handful parsley leaves
- 1 tablespoon pine nuts
- 1 tablespoon grated pecorino cheese
- 2 tablespoons grated Parmesan cheese
- 3 tablespoons extra-virgin olive oil
- Salt, Ground white pepper,

Dressing
- 2 medium eggplants
- 2 large zucchini
- Ground black pepper
- Olive oil
- 3 red cluster tomatoes, sliced
- 3 8-ounce balls of fresh mozzarella, sliced
- 16 thin slices smoked prosciutto (speck)

In a food processor, puree the garlic, basil, parsley, pine nuts, pecorino, and Parmesan cheese. With the machine on, slowly pour in the olive oil and process until just blended. Season with salt and pepper. Set aside.

Heat a grill or grill pan.

Slice the eggplant and zucchini into ¼-inch rounds. Season with salt and black pepper, then drizzle with olive oil. Place the vegetables on the grill for 3 to 4 minutes or until nice grill marks appear on each side and vegetables are cooked through.

Coat a baking sheet with olive oil. Place a layer of eggplant on the bottom, then top each slice with a slice of tomato. Add a slice of the grilled zucchini, then a slice of mozzarella (you will end up with a pyramid shape covered in melted cheese). Bake 5 to 10 minutes, until cheese is melted.

Place the medallions in the center of a large serving platter and sprinkle with pesto sauce. Top with prosciutto. Serve promptly. Serves 8.

Melanzane
alla Parmigiana

❖

Eggplant Parmesan

You've probably had this a million times with regular mozzarella. Fresh mozzarella gives it an update.

- 2 medium eggplants, sliced ¼-inch thick
- Salt, ground white pepper
- 4 tablespoons all-purpose flour
- 1 cup vegetable oil

- 2 cups tomato sauce (see page 74 for recipe)
- 16 thin slices fresh mozzarella
- ½ cup grated Parmesan cheese
- 4 tablespoons basil, julienned

Preheat the oven to 400 degrees F.

Season the eggplant slices with salt and pepper. Cover with flour on both sides then shake gently to remove the excess.

In a deep 12-inch iron skillet, heat the oil over high heat until hot but not smoking. Working in batches, add the eggplant to the pan, 3 to 4 at a time. Cook until brown, flipping once. Remove eggplant from the oil and place on paper towels to drain.

Cover the bottom of a large casserole pan with a thin layer of tomato sauce. Top with a layer of fried eggplant, then with a layer of the mozzarella Sprinkle with Parmesan cheese and basil. Repeat this process twice, placing each layer directly on top of the previous one. Bake for 15 minutes or until the top is brown and bubbly. Serve promptly. Serves 8.

Capesante con Polenta

⇌

Scallops with Polenta

Polenta—ground cornmeal that counts as a whole grain. While you might not want to eat polenta every day, it's a nice change from pasta once in a while and, although you have to stand at the stove and stir polenta, it's still very easy to make.

Polenta
- 4 cups water
- 2 cups polenta
- 2 tablespoons Parmesan cheese
- 1 teaspoon butter
- Salt
- Ground white pepper

Scallops
- 2 tablespoons extra-virgin olive oil, plus more for finishing
- 1 clove garlic, chopped
- 2 shallots, chopped
- 2 tablespoons brandy
- 32 sea scallops

- 2 cups fish broth
- Salt, ground white pepper
- 1 teaspoon butter
- Handful basil, julienned
- 1 cup cherry tomatoes, halved

Bring the water to a boil in a medium saucepan. Add the polenta, and season with salt and ground pepper. Stir for three minutes, then add the cheese and butter. Keep warm.

Heat 2 tablespoons olive oil in a large skillet over medium-high heat. Add the garlic and shallots and cook until golden, about 1 minute. Add the brandy and cook 1 to 2 minutes more. Add the scallops and fish broth to the garlic and shallots. Season with salt and pepper and cook until the scallops are done, about 3 minutes.

Place the polenta in a serving dish. Remove the scallops from the pan with a slotted spoon and place on top of the polenta. Turn up the heat in the pan and quickly reduce the sauce by half. Season again with salt and pepper if necessary.

Add the butter, basil and cherry tomatoes. Cook 1 to 2 minutes more. Spoon the sauce over the polenta and scallops and drizzle with extra virgin olive oil, if desired. Serve promptly. Serves 8.

CROSTINI AL PROSCIUTTO

—◦—

Crostini with Prosciutto

When I tell you that you can put this wonderful appetizer on the table in 10 minutes, I'm not exaggerating. It also makes a great lunch.

- 1 Ciabatta bread, sliced into 8 ⅓-inch pieces
- ½ pound fresh mozzarella cheese, sliced into 8 ¼-inch thick slices

- 8 thin slices prosciutto
- Ground black pepper
- 3 tablespoons chopped Italian parsley

Preheat oven to 375 degrees F.

Arrange the bread on a large baking sheet. Top each piece of bread with a slice of mozzarella. Bake until cheese is melted, 5 to 7 minutes.

Top each piece of bread with a slice of prosciutto. Sprinkle with parsley and pepper. Serve promptly. Serves 8.

CROSTINI
PEPERONATA

◆━◉━◆

Crostini with Peppers

Roasting the peppers in the oven takes a little longer than sautéing them would, but the smoky flavor it gives them is worth the (little) extra effort.

- 2 red bell peppers
- 2 yellow bell peppers
- 2 tablespoons extra-virgin olive oil, plus more for coating peppers
- 1 tablespoon balsamic vinegar
- ½ clove garlic, chopped

- 1 Ciabatta bread, sliced into 8 1/3-inch pieces
- ½ pound fresh mozzarella cheese, sliced into 8 ¼-inch thick slices
- Ground black pepper
- 3 tablespoons chopped Italian parsley

Preheat oven to 375 degrees F.

Lightly coat each bell pepper with olive oil. Place on a baking sheet and roast in the oven, until soft and slightly blackened, about 7-10 minutes. (Turn the peppers while cooking so they cook evenly.)

Remove from the oven and place the peppers in a medium bowl. Cover the bowl with plastic wrap and allow them to cool. Take the peppers out of the bowl and remove their peel and seeds. Slice into ¼-inch strips.

Return the peppers to the bowl and stir in balsamic vinegar, garlic and 2 tablespoons olive oil; set aside.

Arrange the bread on a large baking sheet. Top each piece of bread with a slice of mozzarella. Bake until cheese is melted, 5 to 7 minutes.

Top crostini with pepper mixture. Season with pepper and sprinkle with parsley. Serve right away. Serves 8.

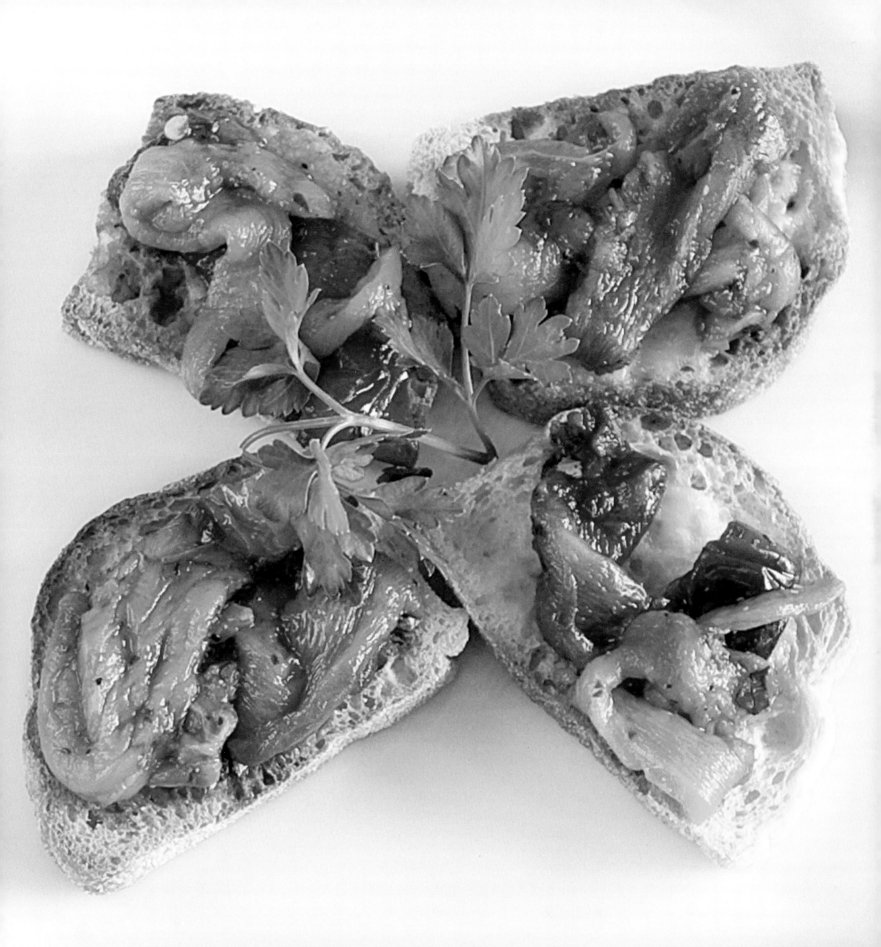

CROSTINI AL FUNGHI

⊰══◉══⊱

Crostini with Mushrooms

Fresh mozzarella is what makes this appetizer so addictive. The good news is that even supermarkets carry fresh mozzarella these days, although if yours doesn't, you can substitute regular mozzarella and still get good results.

- 1 tablespoon extra-virgin olive oil
- 1 clove garlic, chopped
- 3 pounds mushrooms, sliced
- ½ tablespoon white wine
- Salt

- Ground black pepper
- 1 ciabatta bread, sliced into 8 ⅓-inch pieces
- ½ pound fresh mozzarella cheese, sliced into 8 ¼-inch thick slices
- 3 tablespoons chopped Italian parsley

Preheat oven to 375 degrees F.

In a 12-inch nonstick skillet, heat olive oil over medium-high heat. Add garlic and sauté until fragrant, about 30 seconds. Add the mushrooms and sauté until softened, 3 to 4 minutes. Add the wine and increase the heat to high. Cook, stirring, until the liquid evaporates, about 5 minutes. Season with salt and pepper.

Arrange the bread on a large baking sheet. Top each piece of bread with a slice of mozzarella. Bake until cheese is melted, 5 to 7 minutes. Top the crostini, bread with mozzarella, with the mushroom mixture, then sprinkle with parsley. Serve warm. Serves 8.

Bruschetta al
Pomodoro Fresco

—✦═══✦—

Bruschetta with Fresh Tomatoes

This is wonderful as an appetizer or even a light summer lunch.

1 ciabatta bread, sliced into 8 1/3-inch pieces
2 red cluster tomatoes, diced
1 tablespoon extra-virgin olive oil
Salt

Ground black pepper, to taste
1 clove garlic
2 tablespoons julienned basil

Preheat oven to 375 degrees F.

Arrange the bread on a large baking sheet. Bake 3 to 5 minutes, or until lightly brown and crispy.

In a medium bowl, mix the tomatoes and olive oil. Season with salt and pepper.

Gently rub the garlic on one side of each slice of bread. Top the bread with the tomatoes, then sprinkle with basil. Serve promptly. Serves 8.

Zuppa di Pomodoro

Tomato Soup

While olive oil is my go-to fat for cooking, I use a little butter occasionally to cook garlic. Garlic easily burns in olive oil, which can give your whole dish a bitter taste, but if you add a little butter to the pan slows down the cooking. You just need a touch to do the job so no need to worry; it doesn't spoil the healthful quality of the dish.

- 8 organic ripened red cluster tomatoes
- 2 tablespoons extra virgin olive oil
- 1 teaspoon unsalted butter
- 1 clove garlic, chopped
- 2 shallots, chopped
- 1 tablespoon brandy

- 1 sprig fresh rosemary
- Salt, Ground white pepper
- 4 cups water
- Juice of one orange
- 8 slices shaved Parmesan cheese

Cut the tomatoes in half, remove the seeds and dice into small pieces.

Heat the olive oil in a soup pot over medium high heat. Add butter, then the garlic and shallots. When the garlic and shallots are golden, add the brandy and sauté 1 to 2 minutes more. Add the rosemary sprig and tomatoes to the pot. Season with salt and white pepper.

Add the water and bring to a boil. Cook for 5 minutes or until the tomatoes get soft and begin to break down. Remove the rosemary sprig and transfer the soup to a blender (or use an immersion blender). Puree until finely blended. Transfer the soup to a serving bowl and stir in the orange juice. Top with Parmesan cheese and serve promptly. Serves 6-8

ZUPPA DI SPINACI

＊━◯━＊

Spinach Soup

Don't be alarmed when you see that this soup contains cream. It's just a touch and considering that the three tablespoons are divided eight ways, all you're really getting is a teaspoon per serving. Yet a little goes a long way. The cream adds body and richness to the soup. Still, the soup is also delicious without the cream. If you're strictly watching your cholesterol, feel free to omit it.

- 1 pound fresh baby spinach
- 2 tablespoons extra-virgin olive oil
- 1 clove garlic, chopped
- 2 shallots, chopped
- 1 teaspoon unsalted butter
- 1 tablespoon brandy

- 1 sprig fresh rosemary
- 4 cups water
- 3 tablespoons heavy cream, optional
- Salt, Ground white pepper
- 8 slices shaved Parmesan cheese

Bring a large pot of salted water to a boil. Add the spinach and cook for 3 minutes; remove with a slotted spoon.

While spinach is cooking, heat the olive oil in a soup pot over medium-high heat. Add the garlic, shallots, and butter and sauté until golden. Add the brandy, then the rosemary sprig and cook for 1 to 2 minutes more.

Transfer the spinach to the soup pot. Add the water, cream, if desired, and salt and white pepper. Bring to a boil. Cook the soup for 5 minutes more. Remove the rosemary sprig and transfer the soup to a blender (or use an immersion blender). Puree until finely blended. Ladle into serving bowls and top with shaved Parmesan cheese. Serves 6-8

Zuppa Minestrone

⊱━◯━⊰

Vegetable Soup

There is nothing like a steamy bowl of minestrone on a cold winter's evening (though it's light enough to eat in the summer, too). Serve with a hunk of crusty bread.

- ½ cup short pasta or tagliatelle
- 2 tablespoons extra-virgin olive oil
- 1 onion, diced
- 3 carrots, diced
- 1 stalk celery, diced
- 3 russet potatoes, diced

- 4 zucchini, diced
- Salt, ground white pepper
- 2 tablespoons tomato sauce (see page 74 for recipe)
- 2 quarts vegetable broth
- 3 tablespoons julienned basil

Bring a large pot of salted water to boil. Cook pasta until al dente. Drain and set aside.

Heat the olive oil in a soup pot over medium-high heat. Add the onions and cook until lightly browned, about 5 minutes. Add the remaining vegetables and vegetable broth. Season with salt and pepper.

Bring the soup to a boil, then reduce the heat to low. Let simmer for 25 minutes or until the vegetables are tender. Stir occasionally, adding more water if necessary.

Stir in the tomato sauce, and pasta. Garnish with the basil and serve promptly. Serves 8.

RIBOLLITA TOSCANA

❖══◎══❖

Tuscan Ribollita

The amount of time it takes to cook the beans will depend on how fresh they are. Try to buy beans from stores where there is a lot of turnover. If the bag of beans is dusty, evidence that it's been sitting on the shelf for a while, don't buy it. Some farmers markets now sell dried beans; those are a good bet.

- ½ cup pinto beans, soaked overnight and drained
- 2 tablespoons extra-virgin olive oil
- 1 onion, diced
- 3 carrots, diced
- ½ bunch celery, diced

- 1 small green cabbage, julienned
- 3 quarts vegetable broth
- Salt
- Ground white pepper
- 1 loaf ciabatta bread, sliced

Place the pinto beans in a medium soup pot. Add enough water to reach two (2) inches above the beans and bring to a boil. Reduce the heat and let the beans simmer until tender, about 1 hour.

Heat the olive oil in a soup pot over medium-high heat. Add the onions and sauté until lightly browned. Add the beans, carrots, celery, cabbage, and vegetable broth to the pot. Season with salt and pepper. Bring to a boil, then reduce the heat to low.

Stir occasionally, adding water if necessary. Let simmer for 40 minutes or until the vegetables are tender.

Grill or toast the bread until both sides of each slice are browned. Dish the ribollita into bowls and place a slice of bread on top of each. Serve promptly. Serves 8.

ZUPPA DI PESCE

⊷═◉═⊷

Fish Soup

I use salmon in this fish soup, but you can also replace it with your own favorite white fish.

- ½ onion
- 2 small carrots
- 2 stalks celery
- 1 sprig rosemary
- 4 tablespoons extra-virgin olive oil, divided plus more for finishing
- 1 clove garlic, chopped
- 2 shallots, chopped
- 2 tablespoons brandy

- 1 ½ pound salmon, diced
- 8 large shrimp
- 8 sea scallops
- 1 pound squid, sliced
- 3 cups fish broth
- ½ pound Manila clams, scrubbed and rinsed
- ½ pound black mussels, beards removed and rinsed

- 1 ½ cups tomato sauce (see page 74 for recipe)
- ½ tablespoon crushed red chili flakes
- Salt, ground white pepper
- 1 red cluster tomato, diced
- 3 tablespoons chopped Italian parsley

Chop the onion finely in a food processor; set aside. Repeat with the carrots and celery.

Heat 2 tablespoons olive oil in a large skillet over medium heat. Add the onion and sauté until lightly brown. Add the celery, carrots and rosemary and cook over a medium high-heat for 5 minutes. Toss regularly. Set aside.

Heat 2 tablespoons olive oil in a large soup pot over medium-high heat. Add the garlic and shallots.

When they turn golden, add the brandy. Cook for 1-2 minutes more. Add the salmon, shrimp, scallops, squid, and fish broth. Cover and cook for 3 minutes. Add the onion mixture, clams, mussels, tomato sauce and chili flakes, then season with salt and pepper. Cover and cook until the shellfish have just opened, 5 to 7 minutes.

Remove the rosemary, ladle the soup into bowls and garnish with the tomatoes and parsley. Drizzle with olive oil, if desired. Serve promptly. Serves 8.

PRIMI PIATTI
First Course

Salsa di Pomodoro

⬦═◉═⬦

Tomato Sauce

Fresh tomato sauce to have ready. If you don't have any fresh tomatoes, you can use canned tomatoes (though fresh is always my first choice). Here's a quick recipe that uses celery, carrot and onion to help take away the taste of the tin.

Tomato sauce from fresh tomatoes:

- 3 pound ripe red cluster tomatoes
- 1 tablespoon extra-virgin olive oil
- 1 teaspoon unsalted butter
- ½ clove chopped garlic
- ½ shallot, chopped
- 1 teaspoon brandy
- 1 sprig fresh rosemary
- Salt, ground white pepper

Cut the tomatoes in half, remove the seeds, and chop the tomatoes into small pieces.

Heat the olive oil in a soup pot over medium-high heat. Add the butter, then the garlic and shallot and sauté until golden. Add the brandy and cook 1 to 2 minutes more. Add the rosemary sprig and tomatoes, then season with salt and pepper. Add ½ cup water and cook the sauce for 5 minutes or until the tomatoes get soft. Remove the rosemary and transfer the sauce to a blender (or use an immersion blender). Puree until smooth. Makes about 5-6 cups sauce.

Tomato sauce from canned tomatoes:

- 1 28-ounce can whole peeled plum tomatoes (preferably Italian)
- 1 stalk celery
- 1 large carrot
- 1 small onion
- 1 tablespoon unsalted butter
- Salt

Place all ingredients in a soup pot. Bring the mixture to a boil and let simmer for about 10 minutes or until butter is completely dissolved. Remove the celery, carrot and onion. Pass the sauce through a food mill to remove all the tomato seeds. Makes 5-6 cups sauce.

fresh tomato sauce

SALSA ALLA BOLOGNESE

───◦───

Bolognese Sauce

This versatile sauce can be used on any pasta, as well as in lasagna.

- ½ onion
- 2 stalks celery
- 2 small carrots
- 2 sprigs rosemary, leaves chopped
- ¼ cup + 1 tablespoon olive oil
- 4 teaspoons unsalted butter
- 4 cloves garlic, finely chopped

- 4 shallots, chopped
- ½ cup brandy
- 1 teaspoon crushed red chili flakes
- ¼ pound ground pork
- ¼ pound ground beef
- ¼ pound ground veal
- Salt

- Ground white pepper
- 1 cup red wine
- 6 cups tomato sauce
- 1 cup whipping cream
- 1 pound fresh fettuccine

Chop onion finely in a food processor; set aside. Repeat with the celery, then the carrots. Heat 1 tablespoon olive oil in a large skillet over medium heat. Add the onion and sauté until lightly browned. Add the celery, carrots and half of the rosemary and cook over a medium-high heat for 5 minutes. Stir regularly.

Heat oil ¼ cup olive in a large, heavy pot over medium heat. Add the butter, then the garlic and shallots. When the vegetables are golden, add the brandy and cook 1 to 2 minutes more. Add ground beef, pork, veal, chili flakes, and the rest of the rosemary and wine to the pot. Season with salt and pepper. Continue cooking, stirring regularly, until all the liquid has evaporated and the meat is cooked through, about 20 minutes. Add the tomato sauce and cream, and bring to a simmer. Let sauce simmer for 5 minutes.

Makes about 5-6 cups sauce

Pasta Fresca

Fresh Pasta

Making your own pasta by hand at home is a lot easier than you might think. It does take practice, but once you get the hang of it, it's a snap. And it's fun! This pasta can be used in any of the recipes in this book that call for fresh pasta.

Basic pasta
- 1 pound all-purpose flour
- 1 pound durum flour
- 6 large eggs

Spinach pasta
- 1 pound all-purpose flour
- 1/4 pound baby spinach
- 1 pound durum flour
- 6 large eggs

Squid-ink tagliolini
- 1 pound all-purpose flour
- 2 oz. squid ink
- 1 pound durum flour
- 6 large eggs

For all pastas

Place all the ingredients in the bowl of an electric mixer. Beat on low, scraping down the sides of the bowl a couple of times, until the ingredients are well combined.

If you prefer, you can also mix the dough by hand. Place the flour on a flat surface and shape it into a mound. Create a hole in the center, then place the eggs in the hole. Using a fork, begin incorporating the eggs into the flour. Once the ingredients are well combined, use your hands to form a ball.

Spinach pasta

Bring a pot of water to a boil. Add 1/4 pound baby spinach and cook for 3 minutes. Drain well and transfer the spinach to a blender. Add 3 eggs in the fresh pasta recipe and blend to a liquid consistency.

Squid-ink tagliolini

Add 2 oz squid-ink with all ingredients in the bowl of an electric mixer.

A pasta machine is the best option for rolling the dough; otherwise a rolling pin will work just fine. Divide the dough into thirds. Set the slot of the pasta machine to its widest width. Flatten one of the thirds of the dough with the palm of your hand so it is no thicker or wider than the slot of the pasta machine. Start to turn the handle of the pasta machine while feeding the dough into the slot. On the other side hold the flattened dough as it comes out. (Sprinkle some flour over the flattened sheet of pasta to help you manage it better.)

(continues, page 81)

PASTA FRESCA | Fresh Pasta

(continued)

Reduce the slot by one number to the next narrow position. Pass the dough through the pasta machine again. Repeat, narrowing the slot on the pasta machine each time until dough is the desired thickness (it should take 3 times). I recommend about 1/16-inch. Repeat with the other pieces of dough. If you are using a rolling pin, simply continue rolling until you achieve desired thickness (or about 1/16-inch).

After rolling out the dough, it's time to cut the dough into pasta. Most pasta machines come with an adapter that cuts the dough. If you are working on a table, you may wish to cut your dough in half to make it easier to handle.

Decide whether you want to make fettuccine (about 3/8-inch wide), pappardelle (about 5/8-inch wide), lasagna, or some other type of pasta noodles, then feed the dough into the cutting blades or set the sheet of pasta aside for lasagna. Try to have your hand under the center of the cut dough, so you can pick it all up in one bunch.

Alternatively, if you don't have a pasta machine, you can fold the rolled dough into a square. Starting at the open end of the square, cut the dough into strips of desired width.

Immediately after cutting the dough, hang the pasta noodles on a dowel or other object (a clothes drying rack works great). You can also lay the pasta flat on a towel, but it is more likely to stick together.

Cook the pasta right away or keep it in the refrigerator for up to a week.

For lasagna

Bring a pot of salted water to a boil. Cook the pasta sheets for about 3 minutes. Remove pasta sheets from the pot with a slotted spoon and transfer to an ice bath. Drain well on towels and set aside.

GNOCCHI

Gnocchi

Gnocchi—potato dumplings—are a nice alternative to regular pasta. But plan ahead. You will need to cool the potatoes overnight (or at least for several hours).

Plain gnocchi

- 32-ounces potatoes
- 7 ½-ounces all-purpose flour
- 1 egg yolk
- Salt
- 1 pinch ground nutmeg

Place the potatoes in a large pot, cover with water and bring to a boil over high heat. Once boiling, reduce the heat to medium-low and simmer, uncovered, until potatoes are completely tender and just beginning to fall apart, about 25 minutes.

Drain the potatoes in a large colander then cool them overnight in the fridge. Peel and pass through a food mill.

Lay the grated potato on a flat surface. Add the flour, egg yolk, salt and nutmeg. Squeeze all the ingredients together using both hands. Do not overmix!

For both:

Once the ingredients are just combined take a handful of the mixture and roll it into a cylinder about ½-inch thick. Repeat with remaining mixture. Cut each cylinder into ½-inch pieces. Set aside. Serves 8.

Spinach gnocchi

- 32 ounces potatoes
- 4 ounces spinach
- 7 ½-ounces all-purpose flour
- 1 egg yolk
- Salt
- Pinch ground nutmeg

Prepare a steamer. Bring water in the steamer to a boil, add spinach and cook until wilted, about 2 minutes. Transfer the spinach to a blender and puree; set aside.

Lay the grated potato on a flat surface. Add all remaining ingredients including spinach. Mix together using both hands. Do not overmix!

Ravioli di Spinaci

Spinach Ravioli

Ravioli doesn't need an elaborate sauce—there's already so much going on with the filling. This version is topped with a simple sage-white wine sauce.

Pasta
- 1 pound baby spinach
- 1 pound all-purpose flour
- 1 pound durum flour
- 3 large eggs

Filling
- ½ pound cooked spinach (set aside when you're making the pasta)
- 2 egg yolks, divided
- 25 ounces ricotta cheese
- 3 ounces grated Parmesan cheese
- Salt
- Ground white pepper

To make the pasta

Bring a large pot of water to boil. Add the spinach and cook 3 minutes. Drain well and transfer half of the spinach to a blender. (Set aside the remaining spinach for filling).

Add the eggs and blend to a liquid consistency. Place the flour and spinach mixture in the bowl of an electric mixer. Beat on low, scraping down the bowl a couple of times to combine the ingredients well. When a ball forms, remove the dough. (If the dough is too dry, add more egg.)

A pasta machine is the best option for rolling the dough; otherwise a rolling pin will work just fine. Divide the dough into quarters. Set the slot of the pasta machine to its widest width. Flatten one of the thirds of the dough with the palm of your hand so it is no thicker or wider than the slot of the pasta machine.

Start to turn the handle of the pasta machine while feeding the dough into the slot. On the other side, hold the flattened dough as it comes out. (Sprinkle some flour over the flattened sheet of pasta to help you manage it better.) Reduce the slot

(continues, page 86)

by one number to the next narrower position. Pass the dough through the pasta machine again. Repeat, narrowing the slot on the pasta machine each time until dough is desired thickness (it should take 3 times). I recommend about 1/16-inch. Repeat with the other pieces of dough. If you are using a rolling pin, simply continue rolling until you achieve desired thickness. Set the sheets of pasta aside.

To make the filling

In a blender or food processor, puree the cooked spinach until smooth. Transfer it into a large bowl. Add 1 egg yolk, ricotta and Parmesan cheeses. Season with salt and pepper and stir until well combined. Place the filling in a pastry bag, if desired; otherwise using a spoon will work fine.

In a small bowl, mix the remaining egg yolk with 1 teaspoon water; set aside.

To fill the pasta

On a flat surface sprinkled with flour, place one sheet of fresh pasta. As if working on a grid, place about 1 tablespoon of the filling every few inches on the pasta until you have 8 ravioli. Brush all around the filling with the egg wash (this will seal the top layer).

Lay a second sheet of pasta over the first and press down around the filling with your fingers to seal and remove any air pockets. Press down evenly with a rolling pin, then run a sharp knife or pasta cutter along the grid to cut out raviolis. Transfer them to a floured baking sheet and keep in the freezer if not cooking right away. Repeat with the rest of the pasta and filling. Serves 8.

Lune di Melanzane

Eggplant Ravioli

The Bologna-style pink sauce that tops these ravioli is luscious. It's wonderful on plain pasta, too.

Pasta
- 1 pound all-purpose flour
- 1 pound durum flour
- 6 large eggs

Filling
- 1 small eggplant, roughly chopped
- 2 small zucchini, roughly chopped
- 1 tablespoon extra-virgin olive oil
- 1 clove garlic, chopped
- 1 sprig thyme, leaves removed
- Salt, white pepper
- 25 ounces ricotta cheese
- 3 ounces grated Parmesan cheese
- 1 egg yolk

To make the pasta

Place the flour in the bowl of an electric mixer. Beat on low, scraping down the bowl a couple of times to combine the ingredients well. When a ball forms, remove the dough. (If the dough is too dry, add more egg.)

A pasta machine is the best option for rolling the dough; otherwise a rolling pin will work just fine. Divide the dough into quarters. Set the slot of the pasta machine to its widest width. Flatten one of the thirds of the dough with the palm of your hand so it is no thicker or wider than the slot of the pasta machine. Start to turn the handle of the pasta machine while feeding the dough into the slot.

On the other side, hold the flattened dough as it comes out. (Sprinkle some flour over the flattened sheet of pasta to help you manage it better.) Reduce the slot by one number to the next narrower position. Pass the dough through the pasta machine again.

Repeat, narrowing the slot on the pasta machine each time until dough is the desired thickness (it should take 3 times). I recommend about 1/16-inch. Repeat with the other pieces of dough. If you are using a rolling pin, simply continue rolling until you achieve desired thickness. Set the sheets of pasta aside.

To make the filling

Place the eggplant and zucchini in a food processor. Process until finely chopped.

In a small skillet, heat the olive oil over medium-high heat. Add the garlic and cook until golden. Stir in the thyme, eggplant and zucchini. Season with salt and pepper and, stirring frequently, cook until the vegetables are soft, about 10 minutes. Let the mixture cool for 15 minutes.

In a large mixing bowl, combine the vegetable mixture, ricotta and Parmesan cheese. Adjust the seasonings and place the filling in a pastry bag, if desired; otherwise using a spoon will work fine.

Mix the egg yolk with 1 teaspoon water; set aside.

To fill the pasta

On a flat surface sprinkled with flour, place one sheet of fresh pasta. As if working on a grid, place about 1 tablespoon of the filling every few inches on the pasta until you have 8 ravioli. Brush all around the filling with the egg wash (this will seal the top layer).

Lay a second sheet of pasta over the first and press down around the filling with your fingers to seal and remove any air pockets. Press down evenly with a rolling pin, then run a sharp knife or pasta cutter along the grid to cut out raviolis. Transfer them to a floured baking sheet and keep in the freezer if not cooking right away. Repeat with the rest of the pasta and filling. Serves 8.

Ravioli di Zucca

✦━◉━✦

Butternut Squash Ravioli

This dish is particularly lovely in the fall.

Pasta
- 1 pound all-purpose flour
- 1 pound durum flour
- 3 large eggs

Filling
- 1 medium butternut squash
- Canola oil
- 1 tablespoon chopped Italian parsley
- 2 egg yolks, divided
- 3 ounces ricotta cheese
- 2 ounces Parmesan cheese
- Salt
- White pepper

To make the pasta

Place the flour in the bowl of an electric mixer. Beat on low, scraping down the bowl a couple of times to combine the ingredients well. When a ball forms, remove the dough. (If the dough is too dry, add more egg.)

A pasta machine is the best option for rolling the dough; otherwise a rolling pin will work just fine. Divide the dough into quarters. Set the slot of the pasta machine to its widest width. Flatten one of the thirds of the dough with the palm of your hand so it is no thicker or wider than the slot of the pasta machine. Start to turn the handle of the pasta machine while feeding the dough into the slot.

On the other side, hold the flattened dough as it comes out. (Sprinkle some flour over the flattened sheet of pasta to help you manage it better.) Reduce the slot by one number to the next narrowed position. Pass the dough through the pasta machine again.

Repeat, narrowing the slot on the pasta machine each time until dough is desired thickness (it should take 3 times). I recommend about 1/16-inch. Repeat with the other pieces of dough. If you are using a rolling pin, simply continue rolling until you achieve desired thickness. Set the sheets of pasta aside.

To make the filling
Preheat the oven to 400 degrees F. Cut the butternut squash in half, remove the seeds, then coat the flesh with canola oil. Roast until browned, about 45 minutes to 1 hour. Set aside to cool.

When squash is cool enough to handle, remove the skin and cut the squash into chunks. Place in a food processor and process until smooth. Transfer to a large mixing bowl and add the parsley, 1 egg yolk, Parmesan and ricotta cheeses, salt and pepper. Stir until well combined. Place the filling in a pastry bag, if desired; otherwise using a spoon will work fine.

In a small bowl, mix the remaining egg yolk with 1 teaspoon water; set aside.

To fill the pasta
On a flat surface sprinkled with flour, place one sheet of fresh pasta. As if working on a grid, place about 1 tablespoon of the filling every few inches on the pasta until you have 8 ravioli. Brush all around the filling with the egg wash (this will seal the top layer).

Lay a second sheet of pasta over the first and press down around the filling with your fingers to seal and remove any air pockets. Press down evenly with a rolling pin, then run a sharp knife or pasta cutter along the grid to cut out raviolis. Transfer them to a floured baking sheet and keep in the freezer if not cooking right away. Repeat with the rest of the pasta and filling. Serves 8.

Spaghetti Aglio e Olio

※

Spaghetti with Garlic and Olive Oil

To me, this is pure comfort food. Depending on how quickly you can get the water to boil, it takes about 20 minutes to make.

- 1 pound spaghetti
- 4 tablespoons extra-virgin olive oil, plus more for finishing
- 3 cloves garlic, chopped
- ¼ cup white wine

- Pinch crushed red chili flakes
- Handful chopped parsley
- Salt

Bring a large pot of salted water to boil. Cook spaghetti until al dente. Drain.

In the meantime, heat the olive oil in a large saucepan over medium heat. Add the garlic and cook until golden, about 1 minute. Add the wine, and cook 1 to 2 minutes more.

Transfer the pasta to the saucepan. Toss with the chili flakes, parsley, and season with salt. Drizzle with olive oil, if desired. Serve promptly. Serves 8.

Spaghetti
alla Carbonara

Spaghetti Carbonara

This dish is creamy—but it has no cream or butter for that matter. Carbonara is a Roman dish and it should only be made with these ingredients. Adding anything else, including onion and garlic, is an insult to Romans! One of the things that gives it its unique flavor is that the eggs cook from the heat of the pasta. You don't scramble them in a pan, which would make the dish lumpy. Instead, you get pasta that is smooth and silky.

- 1 pound spaghetti
- 8 large eggs
- ½ cup grated Pecorino Romano cheese
- ½ cup grated Parmesan cheese

- 1 teaspoon ground black pepper
- 2 tablespoons extra-virgin olive oil
- 10 ¼-inch slices pancetta, diced
- ½ cup white cooking wine

Bring a large pot of salted water to boil. Cook spaghetti until al dente. Drain.

In the meantime, gently combine the eggs, cheeses and black pepper in a medium bowl. Set aside.

Heat the olive oil in a large saucepan over medium heat. Add the pancetta and cook until it's lightly browned.

Add the white wine, and cook 1 to 2 minutes more. Transfer the spaghetti to the saucepan, and remove from the heat. Pour in the egg-cheese mixture and toss. Serve promptly. Serves 8.

Spaghetti con Pancetta e Ricotta Salata

❖━◦━❖

Spaghetti with Pancetta and Salty Ricotta

This dish actually has three cheeses, but it's the salty ricotta that stands out. Ricotta, pressed and dried, is a variation on the more common, creamy type of ricotta. It has a salty, milky flavor.

- 1 pound spaghetti
- 4 tablespoons extra-virgin olive oil, plus more for finishing
- 3 shallots, diced
- 10 ½-inch slices pancetta, diced
- 1/2 cup white wine
- 1 teaspoon crushed chili flakes
- 1-½ cups tomato sauce (see page 74 for recipe)

- ½ cup grated Parmesan cheese
- ¼ cup grated pecorino cheese
- Salt
- Ground white pepper
- Handful basil, julienned
- 1 cup crumbled salty ricotta

Bring a large pot of salted water to boil. Cook spaghetti until al dente. Drain. In the meantime, heat 4 tablespoons of olive oil in a large saucepan over medium heat. Add the shallots and pancetta. Cook for 1 minute, or until lightly browned. Add the wine, chili flakes and tomato sauce and bring to a simmer. Cook over low heat for 2 minutes. Transfer the pasta to the saucepan.

Add the Parmesan and pecorino cheeses, and season with salt and white pepper. Toss well, then sprinkle with the basil and drizzle with olive oil, if desired. Top with the salty ricotta. Serve promptly. Serves 8.

Spaghetti ai Frutti di Mare

❦

Spaghetti with Seafood

To clean clams and mussels, soak them in cool water for 20 minutes, then scrub them with a brush to remove dirt and debris.

- 1 pound spaghetti
- 4 tablespoons extra-virgin olive oil, plus more for finishing
- 2 cloves garlic, chopped
- 2 tablespoons white wine
- 8 sea scallops (preferably 10-20 count/pound)
- 8 shrimp, shelled and deveined
- ¼ pound sliced squid

- 1 cup fish broth
- 16 Manila clams, cleaned
- 16 black mussels, cleaned
- Pinch crushed chili flakes
- 3 cups tomato sauce (see page 74 for recipe)
- Salt
- 3 tablespoons chopped Italian parsley

Bring a large pot of salted water to boil. Cook spaghetti until al dente. Drain.

In the meantime, heat 4 tablespoons of olive oil in a large deep skillet over medium heat. Add garlic and, stirring, cook until lightly brown, about 1 minute. Add the wine, and cook for 2 to 3 minutes more.

Place the scallops, shrimp, squid and fish broth in the pan, and cook for 3 minutes. Add the clams, mussels, crushed chili flakes and tomato sauce. Season with salt. Cover and cook until the clams and mussels just open up. Transfer the spaghetti to the skillet and toss with the seafood mixture. Finish with the parsley and, if desired, a drizzle of olive oil. Serve promptly. Serves 8.

Spaghetti al Tonno di Blis

❖────◉────❖

Spaghetti with Blis Tuna

Take a break from tuna sandwiches! This is an excellent way to serve tuna, which is rich in disease-preventive omega-3 fatty acids. Whenever possible try to buy Blis tuna that's been hand packed.

- 1 pound spaghetti
- 2 tablespoons extra-virgin olive oil
- 4 anchovy fillets, finely diced
- 2 cloves garlic, chopped
- ½ medium onion medium, chopped
- 20 ounces Blis tuna, lightly rinsed and flaked
- ¼ cup white wine
- 1 basket cherry tomatoes, halved
- Pinch crushed red chili flakes
- Salt
- Handful chopped Italian parsley
- 1 teaspoon oregano

Bring a large pot of salted water to boil. Cook spaghetti until al dente. Drain.

In the meantime, heat the olive oil in a large saucepan over medium-high heat. Add the anchovies, garlic and onion. When lightly browned, add the wine, tuna and cherry tomatoes. Season with the chili flakes and salt. Stir and simmer for 3 to 5 minutes.

Transfer the pasta to a serving bowl and top with the tuna sauce. Add the parsley and oregano and toss. Drizzle with olive oil, if desired, and serve promptly. Serves 8.

Capellini al Pomodoro e Basilico

Capellini with Tomato and Basil

This is about as simple—and as satisfying—as it gets. Capellini, or angel hair pasta is a good alternative to spaghetti when you're pressed for time: it cooks in just three minutes.

- 1 pound Capellini (angel hair)
- 4 tablespoons extra-virgin olive oil, plus more for finishing
- 1 clove garlic, chopped
- Pinch crushed chili flakes

- 4 red cluster tomatoes, diced
- Salt
- ¼ cup grated Parmesan cheese
- Handful basil, julienned

Bring a large pot of salted water to boil. Cook Capellini (mix well so the pasta cooks evenly) until al dente, about 3 minutes. Drain.

In the meantime, heat 4 tablespoons olive oil in a large saucepan over medium heat. Add the garlic. When lightly brown, add the chili flakes and tomatoes and cook 1 to 2 minutes more.

Add the Capellini to the saucepan. Simmer for 2 minutes. Season with salt then add the cheese and basil. Drizzle with olive oil, if desired. Serve promptly. Serves 8.

Linguine con Asparagi e Scarmoza

✦━◉━✦

Linguine with Asparagus and Smoked Mozzarella

At times you want mozzarella to be pleasantly bland (as on pizza). But when you want to give a dish an extra kick, smoked mozzarella is the way to go. It's also great in lasagna.

- 1 pound linguine
- 2 tablespoons extra-virgin olive oil, plus more for finishing
- 2 tablespoons unsalted butter
- 1 clove garlic, chopped
- 1 bunch thin asparagus, cut into 1-inch pieces
- Salt

- 2 tablespoons white wine
- 2 tablespoons grated Parmesan cheese
- 1 cup smoked mozzarella cheese, diced
- Handful basil, julienned
- 12 thin slices smoked prosciutto (speck)

Bring a large pot of salted water to boil. Cook linguine until al dente. Drain.

In the meantime, heat 2 tablespoons of olive oil in a large saucepan over medium heat. Add the butter, then the garlic. When the garlic is lightly browned, add the wine and asparagus. Season with salt and simmer for 2 minutes, or until the asparagus is tender-crisp.

Transfer the linguine to the saucepan. Add the Parmesan, mozzarella cheese, and basil. Toss well. Drizzle with extra virgin olive oil, if desired, and top with smoked prosciutto. Serve promptly. Serves 8.

Linguine
alle Vongole

⟡

Linguine with Clams

Manila clams are your best bet for this recipe, however, if you can't find them, substitute with littleneck clams.

- 1 pound linguine
- 4 tablespoons extra-virgin olive oil, more for finishing
- 3 cloves garlic, chopped
- 1 tablespoon crushed red chili flakes
- ½ cup white wine

- 1 teaspoon butter
- 2 pounds Manila clams
- Salt
- 4 tablespoons Italian, parsley chopped
- 2 red cluster tomatoes, diced

Bring a large pot of salted water to boil. Cook linguine until al dente. Drain.

In the meantime, heat the olive oil in a large saucepan over medium-high heat. Add the garlic and sauté until lightly brown. Add the chili flakes, wine, butter and clams. Season with salt. Cover and cook until the clams just open up, about 7 minutes.

Place the linguine in a large bowl and add the clam sauce. Toss, then garnish with the parsley and tomatoes. Drizzle with extra virgin olive oil if desired and serve promptly. Serves 8.

Linguine Mare e Monti

Linguine with Seafood

If you don't make fish broth yourself (and who does these days?), buy a good quality from your local seafood shop.

- 1 pound linguine
- 4 tablespoons extra-virgin olive oil, more for finishing
- 3 cloves garlic, chopped
- ¼ cup white wine
- 24 Manila clams
- 24 black mussels

- 1 cup porcini mushrooms, diced
- ½ cup fish broth
- Salt
- Pinch of red chili flakes
- 4 tablespoons chopped Italian parsley
- 2 red cluster tomatoes, diced

Bring a large pot of salted water to boil. Cook linguine until al dente. Drain.

In the meantime, heat the olive oil in a large saucepan over medium-high heat. Add the garlic and sauté until lightly brown. Add the wine and cook for 1 to 2 minutes more. Add clams, mussels and porcini mushrooms to the pan. Pour in the fish broth and season with salt and a pinch of chili flakes. Cover and cook until the shells just open up, about 7 minutes.

Place the linguine in a large bowl and add the seafood sauce. Toss, then garnish with the parsley and tomatoes. Drizzle with extra virgin olive oil if desired and serve promptly. Serves 8.

Linguine
con Aragosta

-=◉=-

Linguine with Lobster

Cooking with lobster isn't for the squeamish, but you'll have delicious results if you brave the process.

- 4 live red lobsters
- 1 pound linguine
- 4 tablespoons extra-virgin olive oil, plus more for finishing
- 3 cloves garlic, chopped

- 2 cups fish broth
- 2 baskets cherry tomatoes
- 1 tablespoon crushed red chili flakes
- Salt
- 4 tablespoons chopped Italian parsley

Cut each of the live lobsters in half by plunging a sharp knife in the center of the lobster's head, about 1-1/2 inches down from the eyes. (Alternatively, have the person at the fish counter do it for you.) Crack the lobsters' claws and rinse them lightly. Set aside.

Bring a large pot of salted water to boil. Cook linguine until al dente. Drain.

In the meantime, heat the olive oil in a large saucepan over medium-high heat. Add the garlic. When it's lightly browned, add the lobsters and fish broth to the saucepan. Cover and cook for 5 minutes.

Remove the lobsters from the pan and pull the meat out. Return the meat to the pan, then stir in the cherry tomatoes and chili flakes. Season with salt. Add the drained linguine to the pan. Gently toss. Garnish with the chopped parsley and drizzle with olive oil, if desired. Serve promptly. Serves 8.

Rigatoni all' Amatriciana

Rigatoni Amatriciana

This dish, a staple of Roman menus, originated from Amatrice, a town not far from Rome.

- 1 pound rigatoni
- 4 tablespoons extra-virgin olive oil, plus more for finishing
- 1 clove garlic, chopped
- ½ small onion, finely chopped
- 5 ¼-inch slices pancetta, diced
- 2 tablespoons white wine

- 2 baskets cherry tomatoes, halved
- Pinch crushed red chili flakes
- Pinch ground white pepper
- 1 tablespoon grated pecorino cheese
- 2 tablespoons grated Parmesan cheese
- Handful basil, julienned

Bring a large pot of salted water to boil. Cook rigatoni until al dente. Drain.

In the meantime, heat the olive oil in a large saucepan over medium heat. Add the garlic and onions and stir continuously for 1 minute. Add the pancetta and cook until lightly browned. Add the wine, cherry tomatoes and chili flakes, reduce the heat to low and then simmer for 2 minutes.

Transfer the pasta to the saucepan with the sauce and toss well. Add the pepper, Parmesan and pecorino cheeses and toss again. Sprinkle with basil and, if desired, drizzle with olive oil. Serve promptly. Serves 8.

Penne alla Checca

✦══◉══✦

Penne with Tomato and Mozzarella

Penne alla Checca also makes a great summer dish with diced raw tomatoes.

- 1 pound penne
- 2 tablespoons extra-virgin olive oil, plus more for finishing
- 1 clove garlic, chopped
- Pinch crushed red chili flakes
- 4 red cluster tomatoes, diced
- Salt
- ¼ cup grated Parmesan cheese
- 1 cup diced fresh mozzarella
- Handful basil, julienned

Bring a large pot of salted water to boil. Cook the penne until al dente. Drain.

In the meantime, heat the olive oil in a large saucepan over medium heat. Add the garlic and cook until golden, about 1 minute. Add the chili flakes and tomatoes and simmer for 2 minutes.

Transfer the pasta to the saucepan. Season with salt and top with the Parmesan cheese, mozzarella, and basil. Toss to combine, then drizzle with olive oil, if desired. Serve promptly. Serves 8.

Penne all' Arrabiata

Penne all' Arrabiata

Also known as Angry Pasta

- 1 pound penne
- 4 tablespoons extra-virgin olive oil, plus more for finishing
- 2 cloves garlic, chopped
- 2 tablespoons crushed red chili flakes

- 3 cups tomato sauce (see page 74 for recipe)
- Salt
- 3 tablespoons chopped Italian parsley

Bring a large pot of salted water to boil. Cook the penne until al dente. Drain.

In the meantime, heat the olive oil in a large saucepan over medium heat. Add the garlic and cook until golden, about 1 minute. Add the chili flakes and tomato sauce. Simmer for 2 minutes.

Transfer the pasta to the saucepan. Season with salt and top with the parsley. Toss well, drizzle with extra virgin olive oil, if desired, and serve promptly. Serves 8.

Farfalle con Speck e Rucola

—◦—

Farfalle with Smoked Prosciutto and Arugula

You can spot farfalle by its shape: it looks like bow ties.

- 1 pound farfalle
- 2 tablespoons extra-virgin olive oil, plus more for finishing
- ¼ cup smoked prosciutto, shredded
- 2 tablespoons unsalted butter
- 1 clove garlic, chopped
- 2 shallots, chopped

- 2 teaspoons brandy
- 2 tablespoons chopped Italian parsley
- 8 ounces baby arugula
- ¼ cup diced red cluster tomatoes
- Salt
- Ground white pepper

Bring a large pot of salted water to boil. Cook farfalle until al dente. Drain.

In the meantime, heat the olive oil in a large saucepan over medium high heat. Add the butter, then the smoked prosciutto, garlic and shallots. Sauté until golden the garlic and shallots are golden. Add the brandy and cook 1 to 2 minutes more.

Add the farfalle, parsley, arugula and fresh tomatoes to the pan. Season with salt and pepper. Toss until the pasta is moist. Drizzle with extra virgin olive oil, if desired. Serve promptly. Serves 8.

Orechiette con Funghi e Marsala

—◦═◦—

Orechiette with Mushrooms and Marsala

Orechiette derives from the Italian word for ear, though these noodles look more like little disks.

- 1 pound orechiette
- 2 tablespoons extra-virgin olive oil, plus more for finishing
- 1 teaspoon unsalted butter
- 1 clove garlic, chopped
- ½ cup sweet Marsala wine

- 1 cup small mushrooms, halved
- 2 tablespoons heavy cream
- Salt
- Ground white pepper

Bring a large pot of salted water to boil. Cook orechiette until al dente. Drain.

In the meantime, heat the olive oil in a large saucepan over medium-high heat. Add the butter, then the garlic. Sauté until golden, then add the wine and cook 1 to 2 minutes more.

Add the mushrooms, cream, salt and pepper. Reduce the heat to low and simmer for 7 minutes.

Add the pasta to the mushrooms and gently toss. Drizzle with olive oil, if desired. Serve promptly. Serves 8.

Fusilli con Verdure

Fusilli Pasta with Vegetables

Use this recipe as a template for any pasta and vegetables dish. You can make it with any fresh veggies you have on hand.

- 1 pound fusilli
- 4 tablespoons extra-virgin olive oil, plus more for finishing
- 1 clove garlic, chopped
- 1 onion, diced
- 2 shallots, chopped
- 2 tablespoons brandy

- 1 zucchini, diced
- 2 each red, yellow bell peppers, diced
- 1 small eggplant, diced
- 2 cups tomato sauce (see page 74 for recipe)
- Salt, ground white pepper
- 1 handful basil, julienned

Bring a large pot of salted water to boil. Cook fusilli until al dente. Drain.

In the meantime, heat the olive oil in a large saucepan over medium-high heat. Add the garlic, onions and shallots. When lightly browned, add the cognac and cook 1 to 2 minutes more.

Add zucchini, bell peppers and eggplant to the pan and cook until softened, about 5 minutes. Stir in the tomato sauce and bring to a simmer. Cook for 3 minutes.

Transfer the pasta to the saucepan and toss well with the vegetable sauce, then season with salt and white pepper. Sprinkle with basil and, if desired, drizzle with olive oil. Serve promptly. Serves 8.

Fettuccine alla Bolognese

✦═◉═✦

Fettuccine Bolognese

What distinguishes Bolognese from other types of pastas with meat sauce is the mix of meat. It gets its rich, savory flavor from a combination of pork, beef and veal.

- ½ onion
- 2 stalks celery
- 2 small carrots
- 2 sprigs rosemary, leaves chopped
- ¼ cup + 1 tablespoon olive oil
- 4 teaspoons unsalted butter
- 4 cloves garlic, finely chopped

- 4 shallots, chopped
- ½ cup brandy
- 1 teaspoon crushed red chili flakes
- ¼ pound ground pork
- ¼ pound ground beef
- ¼ pound ground veal
- Salt, Ground white pepper

- 1 cup red wine
- 6 cups tomato sauce (see page 74 for recipe)
- 1 cup whipping cream
- 1 pound fresh fettuccine
- ½ cup grated Parmesan cheese

Chop onion finely in a food processor; set aside. Repeat with the celery, then the carrots. Heat 1 tablespoon olive oil in a large skillet over medium heat. Add the onion and sauté until lightly browned. Add the celery, carrots and half of the rosemary and cook over a medium-high heat for 5 minutes. Stir regularly.

Heat oil ¼ cup olive in a large, heavy pot over medium heat. Add the butter, then the garlic and shallots. When the vegetables are golden add the brandy and cook 1 to 2 minutes more. Add ground beef, pork, veal, chili flakes, rest of the rosemary and wine to the pot. Season with salt and pepper. Continue cooking, stirring regularly, until all the liquid has evaporated and the meat is cooked through, about 20 minutes. Add the tomato sauce and cream, and bring to a simmer. Let sauce simmer for 5 minutes. In the meantime, bring a pot of salted water to a boil. Add the fresh pasta and cook until al dente. Drain and toss with the Bolognese sauce. Sprinkle with the Parmesan cheese and toss again. Serve promptly. Serves 8.

Fettuccine al Salmone

Fettuccine with Salmon

- 1 pound fresh fettuccine
- 2 pounds wild salmon, cut into ··-inch pieces
- Salt, Ground white pepper
- 1 tablespoon all-purpose flour
- 1 tablespoon extra-virgin olive oil, plus more for finishing
- 4 teaspoons unsalted butter
- 1 clove garlic, chopped

- 1 shallot, chopped
- 1 small leek, finely chopped
- 2 tablespoons brandy
- 1 cup fish broth
- 2 cups tomato sauce (see page 74 for recipe)
- ½ cup whipping cream
- 4 tablespoons chopped Italian parsley

Rinse and dry diced salmon. Season with salt and pepper, then gently toss with the flour.

In a large skillet, heat the olive over high heat. Add the butter, then the garlic, shallot and leek. When golden, add the brandy and cook 1 to 2 minutes more. Add the salmon, fish broth, tomato sauce and cream.

Reduce the heat to medium, simmer for 5 minutes, stirring occasionally, or until the salmon is cooked through.

In the meantime, bring a pot of salted water to a boil. Add the fresh pasta and cook until al dente. Drain and toss with the salmon. Sprinkle with chopped parsley and drizzle with olive oil, if desired. Serve promptly. Serves 8.

Fettuccine allo Scoglio

Fettuccine with Shellfish

I like to use fresh fettucine in this dish, but dried works well, too.

- 1 pound fresh fettuccine
- 4 tablespoons extra-virgin olive oil, plus more for finishing
- 3 cloves garlic, chopped
- ½ cup white wine
- 8 large uncooked shrimp, shelled and deveined
- 8 sea scallops
- 24 Manila clams

- 24 black mussels
- 1 teaspoon crushed red chili flakes
- 2 cups fish broth
- Salt
- Ground white pepper
- 3 tablespoons chopped Italian parsley
- ½ cup diced red cluster tomato

Bring a large pot of salted water to boil. Cook fettuccine until al dente. Drain.

In the meantime, heat the olive oil in a large saucepan over medium high heat. Add the garlic. Sauté until lightly brown, then add the wine and cook 1 to 2 minutes longer.

Add the shrimp and scallops to the pan and cook thoroughly, about 3 to 5 minutes. Add the clams, mussels, fish broth, crushed chili flakes and season with salt and pepper. Cover and cook until the clams and mussels just open up, about 5 minutes. Add the fettuccine, parsley and tomato to the pan and toss. Drizzle with olive oil, if desired. Serve promptly. Serves 8.

Tagliatelle alla Fiorentina

⊶⊙⊶

Tagliatelle Fiorentina

Tagliatelle is a Northern Italian noodle, shaped like a long flat ribbon, similar to (but usually a little narrower than) fettucine.

- 1 pound fresh tagliatelle
- 2 tablespoons extra-virgin olive oil
- 2 cloves garlic, chopped
- ½ cup prosciutto, diced
- 2 tablespoons win
- 1 cup sliced mushrooms

- ½ cup peas
- 2 cups heavy cream
- 1 teaspoon butter
- Salt, Ground white pepper
- ½ cup grated Parmesan cheese

Bring a large pot of salted water to boil. Cook tagliatelle until al dente. Drain.

In the meantime, heat the olive oil in a large saucepan over medium heat. Add the garlic and prosciutto, and sauté until lightly browned, about 1 minute. Add the wine, mushrooms, peas, cream and butter. Reduce the heat to low and simmer for 3 minutes.

Add the tagliatelle to the sauce in the pan. Season with salt and pepper, and toss with the Parmesan cheese. Serve promptly. Serves 8.

TAGLIOLINI AL GRANCHIO

✦⟾⟾✦

Tagliolini with Crabmeat

Tagliolini is a thin flat noodle. This recipe calls for spinach tagliolini, but plain noodles are fine, too.

- 1 pound spinach tagliolini
- 4 live yellow crabs
- 2 tablespoons extra-virgin olive oil, plus more for finishing
- 2 cloves garlic, chopped
- 1 tablespoon crushed red chili flakes

- 1 cup fish broth
- 2 baskets cherry tomatoes
- 2 cups tomato sauce (see recipe, page 74)
- Salt
- 2 tablespoons chopped Italian parsley

Bring two pots of salted water to boil. In one, cook the tagliolini until al dente. Drain.

In the other pot, cook the crabs for 5 to 8 minutes. Let cool, then crack the crab's claws and lightly rinse. Twist off the remaining legs, crack them, then remove as much crabmeat as possible from the claws and legs. Set aside.

In a large saucepan, heat the olive oil over medium-high heat. Add the garlic and sauté until golden. Add the crabmeat, chili flakes, fish broth, cherry tomatoes and tomato sauce. Season with salt. Cook for 2 minutes.

Add the tagliolini to the sauce in the pan. Toss with the parsley and, if desired, drizzle with olive oil. Serve promptly. Serves 8.

TAGLIOLINI CON
GAMBERI E RUCOLA

⊷⚬⚬⊶

Tagliolini with Shrimp and Arugula

Arugula and shrimp are a great combination. The sharpness of the lettuce contrasts nicely against the shellfish's briny flavor.

- 1 pound fresh tagliolini (see recipe, page 78)
- 2 tablespoons extra-virgin olive oil, plus more for finishing
- ½ pound baby arugula
- 1 teaspoon butter
- 1 clove garlic, chopped
- 2 shallots, chopped
- 2 tablespoons chopped Italian parsley

- 2 red cluster tomatoes, diced
- 2 tablespoons brandy
- 32 shrimp, shelled and deveined
- 1 cup fish broth
- Salt
- Ground white pepper
- Arugula sauce (see recipe, page 65)

Heat the olive oil in a large saucepan over medium-high heat. Add the butter, then the garlic and shallots and sauté until golden. Add the brandy and cook 1 to 2 minutes more. Add the shrimp, fish broth, and season with salt and pepper. Simmer for 5 minutes or until shrimp are cooked through.

In the meantime, bring a pot of salted water to a boil. Cook the tagliolini until al dente, drain and add to the sauce. Toss, then add the arugula and tomato and toss again. Transfer to a serving bowl and sprinkle with chopped parsley.

Optional arugula sauce, for plating:
See spinach soup recipe, page 65. Substitute arugula for spinach and omit the cheese.

To serve: Pour ¼ cup of fresh arugula sauce onto a serving plate, then place tagliolini con gamberi on top. Drizzle with olive oil if desired. Serve promptly. Serves 8.

Pappardelle con Sugo di Pollo

⁌⦿⁍

Pappardelle with Chicken Sauce

This is one of the more indulgent pastas I serve at Trattoria Mollie, but the creamy tomato sauce is worth the extra calories!

- 1 pound fresh pappardelle pasta
- ½ onion
- 2 stalks celery
- 2 small carrots
- 4 tablespoons extra-virgin olive oil, divided, plus more for finishing

- 2 sprigs rosemary, divided, leaves removed and chopped
- 2 cloves garlic, chopped
- 2 shallots, chopped
- 4 tablespoons brandy
- 1 tablespoon crushed red chili flakes

- 4 organic boneless chicken breasts
- 2 cups chicken broth
- 3 cups tomato sauce (see recipe, page 74)
- 1 cup whipping cream
- Salt, ground white pepper
- Grated Parmesan cheese

Bring a large pot of salted water to boil. Cook the pappardelle until al dente. Drain.

In the meantime, chop the onion finely in a food processor; set aside. Repeat with the celery, then the carrots. Heat 2 tablespoons olive oil in a large skillet over medium heat. Add the onion and sauté until lightly browned. Add the celery, carrots and half of the rosemary and cook over a medium-high heat for 5 minutes. Stir regularly.

In a large saucepan, heat the remaining 2 tablespoons olive oil over medium-high heat. Add the garlic, shallots and sauté until golden. Add the brandy and cook 1 to 2 minutes more. Stir in the remaining rosemary and chili flakes, then place the chicken breasts in the pan. Season with salt and pepper. Add the chicken broth, reduce the heat and simmer for 10 minutes, or until the chicken is cooked all the way through. Add the tomato sauce and cream.

Transfer the pasta to pan with the chicken sauce. Toss well. Garnish with Parmesan cheese and a drizzle with olive oil, if desired. Serve promptly. Serves 8.

Pappardelle
con Scampi e Asparagi

❖

Pappardelle with Prawns and Asparagus

Choose asparagus that are neither too fat nor too thin. Stalks sized somewhere in the middle will match the shrimp's cooking time.

- 1 pound fresh pappardelle pasta (see recipe, page 78)
- 2 tablespoons olive oil, plus more for finishing
- 4 tablespoons unsalted butter
- 1 clove garlic, chopped
- 1 shallot, chopped
- 2 tablespoons brandy
- 16 large uncooked shrimp, peeled and deveined

- 1 cup fish broth
- 1 bunch asparagus, cut into 2-inch pieces
- Pinch crushed red chili flakes
- Salt
- Ground white pepper
- 2 tablespoons chopped Italian parsley
- 2 cups fresh tomato sauce (see recipe, page 74)

Bring a large pot of salted water to boil. Cook the pappardelle until al dente. Drain.

While the pasta cooks, heat the olive oil in a large saucepan over medium high heat. Add the butter, then the garlic and shallots. Sauté until lightly brown, then add the brandy and cook 1 to 2 minutes more. Add shrimp, fish broth, asparagus and chili flakes. Season with salt and pepper. Cook until shrimp are done and asparagus is tender crisp, about 3 minutes.

Add the pasta to the pan and toss to moisten.

For plating, pour ¼ cup of fresh tomato sauce onto a serving plate, then place pappardelle con scampi on top. Garnish with parsley and drizzle with olive oil, if desired. Serve promptly. Serves 8.

Tagliolini Neri
con Calamari

❖═◗❖

Squid-Ink Tagliolini with Calamari

- 1 pound squid-ink pasta *(see recipe, page 78)*
- 2 tablespoons extra- virgin olive oil, plus more for finishing
- 1 teaspoon butter
- 1 clove garlic, chopped
- 2 shallots, chopped
- 2 tablespoons brandy
- 1 pound T&T ocean pearl squid, tubes and tentacles, julienne

- 1 cup fish broth
- Salt, to taste
- Ground white pepper, to taste
- 2 tablespoons chopped Italian parsley
- 2 red cluster tomatoes, diced

For plating:
- 2 cups tomato sauce (see recipe, page 74)

Heat the olive oil in a large saucepan over medium-high heat. Add the butter, then the garlic and shallots and sauté until golden. Flambé with brandy, then add squid, fish broth, and season with salt and pepper. Simmer for 5 minutes or until squid is cooked through.

In the meantime, bring a pot of salted water to a boil. Cook the tagliolini until al dente, drain and add to the sauce. Toss, then add the tomatoes and parsley and toss again.

To serve: Pour ¼ cup of tomato sauce onto a dinner plate then transfer tagliolini on top. Drizzle with olive oil if desired. Serve promptly. Serves 8.

Polpette alla Mollie

Mollie's Meatballs

These meatballs, a favorite of Oprah's, were featured in her magazine and on her TV show.

- 2 cups vegetable oil
- 1 pound hot Italian turkey sausage, removed from its casings
- 12 ounces fresh breadcrumbs, divided
- 5 eggs, divided
- 2 ounces Parmesan cheese, plus extra for garnish
- 2 tablespoons whipping cream
- 2 tablespoons chopped Italian parsley, divided
- 1 teaspoon + 1 pinch crushed red pepper flakes
- Salt
- Ground white pepper
- 3 ounces raisins
- ½ cup all-purpose flour
- 1 tablespoon extra-virgin olive oil
- 2 cloves garlic, hopped
- ⅔ cup shallots, chopped
- 1 tablespoon brandy
- 4 cups tomato sauce (see recipe, page 74)
- 1 tablespoon oregano, chopped

Preheat the oven to 400 degrees F. Place the vegetable oil in a deep fryer or large, heavy pot and heat to 400 degrees F. In a large bowl, combine the sausage, 2 ounces breadcrumbs, 1 egg, 2 ounces Parmesan cheese, cream, 1 tablespoon Italian parsley, crushed red pepper flakes and a pinch of salt and pepper. Gently mix together to distribute seasonings. Add the raisins and mix again. Shape the meat into meatballs slightly smaller than a golf ball. Set aside.

Place the flour in a shallow bowl. In another bowl, beat four eggs. In a third bowl, place the remaining breadcrumbs. Roll the meatballs in the flour, dip them into the egg wash, then roll them in the breadcrumbs, coating them evenly.

Using a slotted spoon, transfer the meatballs to the deep fry and fry until golden, about one minute. Remove from the oil with a slotted spoon and drain the meatballs on a paper towel-lined plate.

In a large ovenproof saucepan, heat the olive oil over medium-high heat. Add the garlic and shallots, and sauté until golden. Stir in a pinch of red pepper, add the brandy and cook 1 to 2 minutes more. Add the tomato sauce and transfer the meatballs into the pan, covering them with sauce. Put the pan into the oven and cook until the meatballs are cooked through, about 20 minutes.

Garnish the meatballs with the remaining tablespoon of parsley, the oregano and Parmesan cheese. Serve promptly, alone or with pasta. Serves 8.

Gnocchi alla Sorentina

Gnocchi with Tomato and Basil

Gnocchi—potato dumplings—are a nice alternative to regular pasta. But plan ahead. Just remember to cool the potatoes overnight (or at least for several hours).

- 4 tablespoons extra-virgin olive oil
- 1 clove garlic, chopped
- 1 pinch crushed chili flakes
- 3 cups tomato sauce (see recipe, page 74)

- Salt
- Parmesan cheese
- ½ cup fresh mozzarella, diced
- ½ cup julienned basil

Set aside the gnocchi. (See gnocchi recipe on page 82)

Heat the olive oil in a large saucepan over medium heat. Add the garlic and sauté until lightly browned. Add the chili flakes and tomato sauce. Simmer for 2 minutes.

In the meantime, bring a large pot of salted water to a boil. Add the gnocchi to the pot. Remove each with a slotted spoon as soon as it floats to the surface.

Add the gnocchi to the sauce and toss gently. Top with Parmesan cheese, fresh mozzarella, basil and, if desired, a drizzle of extra virgin olive oil. Serve promptly. Serves 8.

Ravioli di Spinaci

⋯⟁⋯

Spinach Ravioli

Ravioli doesn't need an elaborate sauce—there's already so much going on with the filling. This version is topped with a simple sage-white wine sauce.

- 2 tablespoons extra-virgin olive oil
- 1 clove garlic, chopped
- 1 tablespoon unsalted butter
- 2 tablespoons sage

- 2 tablespoons white wine
- Salt
- 3 tablespoons grated Parmesan cheese

For fresh spinach ravioli, see recipe on page 85.

Heat the olive oil in a large saucepan over medium heat. Add the garlic and cook until lightly browned. Add the butter, sage and wine. Simmer for 2 minutes. Season with salt.

In the meantime, bring a pot of salted water to a boil. Cook the ravioli until al dente. Remove the ravioli from the pot with a slotted spoon and transfer it to the saucepan with the sauce. Gently toss. Garnish with Parmesan cheese and serve promptly. Serves 8.

LUNE DI MELANZANE

❦

Eggplant Ravioli

The Bologna-style pink sauce that tops these ravioli is luscious. It's wonderful on plain pasta, too.

- 2 tablespoons extra-virgin olive oil
- 1 clove garlic, chopped
- 1 sprig thyme, leaves removed
- 2 tablespoons white wine

- 2 cups tomato sauce (see recipe, page 74) or best-quality store bought
- 2 tablespoons heavy cream
- Salt
- 3 tablespoons grated Parmesan cheese

Set aside the ravioli. (See eggplant ravioli recipe, page 88)

Heat the olive oil in a large saucepan over medium heat. Add the garlic and cook until lightly browned. Add the thyme, wine, tomato sauce and cream to the pan and bring to a simmer. Simmer for 4 minutes. Season with salt.

In the meantime, bring a pot of salted water to a boil. Cook the ravioli until al dente. Remove the ravioli from the pot with a slotted spoon and transfer to the saucepan with the sauce. Gently toss. Garnish with Parmesan cheese and serve promptly. Serves 8.

Ravioli di Zucca

⊶═◉═⊷

Butternut Squash Ravioli

This dish is particularly lovely in the fall.

- 2 tablespoons extra-virgin olive oil
- 1 clove garlic, chopped
- 1 tablespoon unsalted butter
- 2 tablespoons sage

- 2 tablespoons white wine
- Salt
- 3 tablespoons grated Parmesan cheese

For fresh butternut squash ravioli, see recipe on page 90.

Heat the olive oil in a large saucepan over medium heat. Add the garlic and cook until lightly browned. Add the butter, sage and wine. Simmer for 2 minutes. Season with salt.

In the meantime, bring a pot of salted water to a boil. Cook the ravioli until al dente. Remove the ravioli from the pot with a slotted spoon and transfer it to the saucepan with the sauce. Gently toss. Garnish with Parmesan cheese and serve promptly. Serves 8.

LASAGNE

⋯⊨⊏⋯

Lasagna

- 6 cups Bolognese sauce (see recipe, page 77)
- Fresh spinach pasta (see recipe, page 85)

Besciamella sauce
- 5 tablespoons all purpose flour
- 6 tablespoons unsalted butter
- Salt, to taste
- Ground white pepper, to taste

- Ground nutmeg, 1 pinch
- 4 cups whole milk

To assemble
- 1 cup grated Parmesan cheese
- 1 teaspoon unsalted butter

Besciamella

In a medium saucepan, heat milk on low heat. In a separate saucepan, heat butter until melted. Add flour and stir for 3 minutes. Slowly whisk the butter and flour mixture into the milk, then season with salt, pepper and nutmeg. Cook until very smooth and bring to a boil. Set aside.

Assemble

Cover the bottom of a 9 x 13-inch baking pan with 1 teaspoon butter. Spread 1 cup of Bolognese sauce and 1/3 cup of besciamella sauce in the bottom of the pan. Top with 1

tablespoon of Parmesan cheese. Place a sheet of pasta on top of the sauce. Continue building the lasagne until you have 5 layers. Finish with a top layer of sauce and Parmesan. I recommended letting the lasagna settle over night. Cut into servings before baking in the oven at 375 degrees F for about 25 to 30 minutes, or until it starts to brown. Serves 10.

RISOTTO
AI FUNGHI PORCINI

✦═══◆═══✦

Risotto with Porcini Mushrooms

Risotto, it's no secret, requires patience. You have to stand at the stove and stir it constantly. But rather than finding it a chore, I enjoy it. It's a nice time to just relax and let your mind wander (although not too much—you don't want to end up with scorched rice!)

- 2 cups porcini mushrooms
- 4 tablespoons extra-virgin olive oil, plus more for finishing
- 1 teaspoon + 1 tablespoon unsalted butter
- 2 cloves garlic, chopped
- 2 shallots, chopped

- 3 tablespoons brandy
- 4 cups Arborio rice
- Salt, ground white pepper
- 4-6 cups vegetable broth
- 3 tablespoons chopped Italian parsley

Dice the porcini mushrooms. Collect any juice they release and set aside.

In a large heavy pot, heat the olive oil over medium-high heat. Add 1 teaspoon butter, then the garlic and shallots. When golden, add the brandy and cook 1 to 2 minutes more.

Add the porcini mushrooms, porcini juice and rice to the pot. Season with salt and pepper. Reduce the heat to medium and, stirring constantly with a wooden spoon, add ¼ cup tomato sauce and the cream. Continue stirring, then when

the rice has absorbed the liquid, add · cup broth. When the broth is absorbed, repeat, then continue cooking, stirring and adding broth in ½ cup measures as it's absorbed, until the rice is tender but al dente, about 15 to 20 minutes. Stir in 1 tablespoon butter and the parsley and season again if necessary. Drizzle with olive oil if desired. Serve promptly. Serves 8.

Risotto con Asparagi

Risotto with Asparagus

Instead of cooking the rice with broth as per usual when you make risotto, in this recipe you use pureed asparagus. It makes for a very flavorful outcome.

- 3 bunches asparagus
- 3 tablespoons extra-virgin olive oil, plus more for finishing
- 1 teaspoon + 1 tablespoon unsalted butter
- 1 clove garlic, chopped

- 1 shallot, chopped
- 1 tablespoons brandy
- 1 sprig rosemary
- 1 tablespoon heavy cream
- Salt
- Ground white pepper

- 4 cups Arborio rice
- 4 tablespoons grated Parmesan cheese
- 3 tablespoons chopped Italian parsley

Trim the ends of the asparagus. Slice one bunch of asparagus at a 45 degree angle into ¼-inch pieces; set aside. Bring a pot of salted water to a boil and cook the remaining bunches of the asparagus until soft, about 5 minutes.

In the meantime, heat 1 tablespoon of olive oil in a medium saucepan. Add 1 teaspoon of butter, then the garlic and shallots. When golden, add the brandy and the rosemary sprig and cook 1 to 2 minutes more.

Transfer the cooked asparagus to the saucepan. Add 1 cup water, the cream and a pinch of salt and pepper. Cook the ingredients for 3 minutes to incorporate flavors. Remove the rosemary sprig and bring the mixture to a blender. Puree until smooth; set aside.

Heat a large heavy pot over medium-high heat.

Add the risotto, sliced asparagus and half of the pureed asparagus sauce. Season with salt and white pepper. Reduce the heat to medium and stir constantly with a wooden spoon until the rice has absorbed the liquid.

Continue cooking and stirring, adding more broth in 1/2 cup measures as it's absorbed, until the rice is tender but al dente, about 15 minutes.

Stir in 1 tablespoon butter, the cheese and the parsley and season again if necessary. Drizzle with olive oil if desired. Serve promptly. Serves 8.

RISOTTO ALLA
CREAMA DI SCAMPI

Risotto with Prawns

Fish broth gives this dish pungency. If it's too much for you, substitute vegetable broth.

- 3 tablespoons extra-virgin olive oil, plus more for finishing
- 3 cloves garlic, chopped
- 3 tablespoon white wine
- 16 raw shrimp, peeled and deveined
- 4 cups Arborio rice
- 4 cups fish broth
- Pinch crushed red chili flake

- Salt
- Ground white pepper
- ½ cup tomato sauce (see recipe, page 74)
- ¼ cup heavy cream
- 1 tablespoon unsalted butter
- 3 tablespoons chopped Italian parsley

In a large heavy pot, heat the olive oil over medium-high heat. Add the garlic and sauté until lightly browned. Add the wine and cook 1 to 2 minutes more.

Add the shrimp, risotto and 2 cups fish broth to the pan. Season with chili flakes, salt and pepper. Reduce the heat to medium and, stirring constantly with a wooden spoon, cook until the rice has absorbed the liquid. Add the tomato sauce and cream and stir until absorbed. Adtd 1/2 cup more of the fish broth.

Continue cooking and stirring, adding more broth in 1/2 cup measures as it's absorbed, until the rice is tender but al dente, about 15 minutes.

Stir in the butter and parsley and season again if necessary. Drizzle with olive oil if desired. Serve promptly. Serves 8.

Risotto con Granchio

❖⊑⊒❖

Risotto with Crabmeat

There's nothing quite like fresh crabmeat, but if you're squeamish, buy crabmeat from your local seafood shop.

- 4 live yellow crabs
- 4 tablespoons extra-virgin olive oil, plus more for finishing
- 1 clove garlic, chopped
- 4 cups Arborio rice
- 3-5 cups fish broth

- Pinch crushed red chili flakes
- 1 cup cherry tomatoes, halved
- Ground white pepper
- Salt
- 1 tablespoon unsalted butter
- 3 tablespoons chopped Italian parsley

Bring a pot of salted water to a boil. Cook the crabs for 5 to 8 minutes. Let cool, then crack the crab's main claws and lightly rinse. Crack the small claws, then remove as much crabmeat as possible from the claws. Set aside.

In a large saucepan, heat the olive oil over medium-high heat. Add the garlic and sauté until golden. Add the risotto and 2 cups of fish broth to the pan. Season with the chili flakes, salt and pepper. Reduce the heat to medium and, stirring constantly with a wooden spoon, cook until the fish broth is absorbed.

Add the crabmeat and $\frac{1}{2}$ cup fish broth. Continue cooking and stirring, adding more broth in $\frac{1}{2}$ cup measures as it's absorbed. Cook until the rice is tender, but al dente, about 8 or 10 more minutes. Add the cherry tomatoes and cook for 1 to 2 minutes to allow them to soften. Stir in the butter and parsley and season again if necessary. Drizzle with olive oil if desired. Serve promptly. Serves 8.

Risotto con Aragosta

⟞⟐⟐⟞

Risotto with Lobster

Spiny lobsters are lobsters that lack claws. The meat is firm and sweet. They're available October through March. If you can't find them, use rock lobster tails or regular lobsters.

- 4 live spiny lobsters
- 4 tablespoons extra-virgin olive oil, plus more for finishing
- 1 clove garlic, chopped
- 4 cups Arborio rice
- 3-5 cups fish broth

- Pinch crushed red chili flakes
- 1 cup cherry tomatoes, halved
- Ground white pepper
- Salt
- 1 teaspoon unsalted butter
- 3 tablespoons chopped Italian parsley

Bring a pot of salted water to a boil. Cook the lobsters for 5 to 8 minutes. Let cool, then cut down through the head of the lobster with a sharp knife. Repeat from the opposite end to cut through the rest of the body. Rinse and devein. Remove the lobster meat, coarsely chop, and set aside.

In a large saucepan, heat the olive oil over medium-high heat. Add the garlic and sauté until golden. Add the risotto and 2 cups of the fish broth to the pan. Season with the chili flakes and salt and pepper. Reduce the heat to medium and, stirring constantly with a wooden spoon, cook until the fish broth is absorbed, about 10 minutes.

Add the lobster meat and $\frac{1}{2}$ cup fish broth. Continue cooking and stirring, adding more broth in $\frac{1}{2}$ cup measures as it's absorbed. Cook until the rice is tender, but al dente, about 8 or 10 more minutes. Add the cherry tomatoes and cook 1 to 2 minutes to allow them to soften. Stir in the butter and parsley and season if necessary. Drizzle with olive oil, if desired. Serve promptly. Serves 8.

Risotto con Calamari

※

Risotto with Calamari

Choose squid that are small and whole with clear eyes.

- 1 pound squid
- 3 tablespoons extra-virgin olive oil
- 2 tablespoons unsalted butter, divided
- 3 cloves garlic, chopped
- 2 shallots, chopped
- 1 tablespoon brandy
- 4 cups Arborio rice

- 6-8 cups fish broth
- Pinch crushed red chili flakes
- Salt
- Ground white pepper,
- 1 cup cherry tomatoes, halved
- 3 tablespoon chopped Italian parsley

Slice the squid tubes into small rings and halve the heads. Rinse and dry; set aside. In a large saucepan, heat the olive oil over medium high-heat. Add 1 tablespoon butter, then the garlic and shallots. When lightly browned, add the brandy and cook 1 to 2 minutes more. Add the risotto and 2 cups of the fish broth to the pan. Season with the chili flakes, salt and pepper. Reduce the heat to medium and, stirring constantly with a wooden spoon, cook until the fish broth is absorbed.

Add the calamari and ½ cup fish broth. Continue cooking and stirring, adding more broth in ½ cup measures as it's absorbed. Cook until the rice is tender, but al dente, about 8 or 10 more minutes. Add the cherry tomatoes and cook 1 to 2 minutes to allow them to soften. Stir in the butter and parsley and season if necessary. Drizzle with olive oil, if desired. Serve promptly. Serves 8.

Risotto alla Pescatora

Risotto with Seafood

This is a seafood lover's delight. Serve it with a crisp white wine.

- 3 tablespoons extra-virgin olive oil, plus more for finishing
- 2 cloves garlic, chopped
- 2 tablespoon white wine
- 8 raw shrimp, peeled and deveined
- 6 large sea scallops
- ½ pound squid, sliced
- 3 cups fish broth
- Pinch crushed red chili flakes

- 16 Manila clams, cleaned and rinsed
- 16 mussels, beards removed and rinsed
- 4 cups Arborio rice
- 1 ½ cups tomato sauce
- Salt
- Ground white pepper,
- 1 tablespoon unsalted butter
- 3 tablespoons chopped Italian parsley

In a large heavy pot, heat the olive oil over medium-high heat. Add the garlic and sauté until lightly browned. Add the wine and cook 1 to 2 minutes more.

Add the shrimp, sea scallops, squid and risotto to the pan. Add the fish broth, then season with the chili flakes, salt and pepper. Reduce the heat to medium, and add the tomato sauce.

Stirring constantly with a wooden spoon, cook until the rice has absorbed the liquid. Add ½ cup more fish broth, then the clams and mussels.

Continue cooking and stirring, adding fish broth in ½ cup measures as it's absorbed, until the rice is tender but al dente and the shellfish have opened, about 15 minutes.

Stir in the butter and parsley and season again if necessary. Drizzle with olive oil if desired. Serve promptly. Serves 8.

Acknowledgments

Thank you, first and foremost to my husband, Bob Ahlstrand, for his endless support and sacrifices in support of my dream. I am very grateful to you. Great appreciation and thanks to my son, Ali, who goes out of his way to help me with the restaurant. You are always there to protect me and do the utmost to handle my emotions. Thanks to all my family in America and Ethiopia, who have always supported, encouraged and believed in me. Thanks to my father and mother for being proud of me. Although my dad was a victim of a society that told him not to let his kids be independent, I have always known that deep inside he believed in education and was proud of my independence. It's hard for a man to have a daughter who is not like other Muslim girls, but I knew through the look in his eyes and his smile that he was on my side. Thank you to my partners in Trattoria Mollie for your support and for being advocates of the business. I am grateful that you have been such loyal partners and customers. Likewise, thank you to all my wonderful customers from near and far. Without your support, all this would not be possible. I have a great love and appreciation for my guys in the kitchen and dining room. Thank you so much for your loyalty, honesty, organization, teamwork and overall hard work. Without you guys I wouldn't be here. Eduardo Carranza, Julio Carranza, Juan Carlos Carranza—you are not only my employees, you are my kids! We've been together 17 years. Francisco Castro, I love you for protecting me and making my life easier. Signor, I care so much about you. If I get rich, I'll buy you a house! Thank you, too, to, Sebastian and Felipe, for getting the job done in the kitchen. You are a great team. Great thanks as well to the dining room staff: Monica Bevinetto Hathaway, Paola Patturelli Hill, Guillermo Gutierrez and all my former staff, some of whom are still in the U.S. and some of whom went back to Italy. It was nice to work with you.

Ringrazio:
- La famiglia Vissani per avermi insegnato a riconoscere e preparare I mighliori Tartufi Bianchi il pesce fresco.
- Arturo, per avermi svelato I misteri della Cucina Romana.
- Roberta di Bologna per avermi insegnato a preparare la pasta fresca.
- Angelo per avermi insegnato come preparare la ciabatta.
- La famiglia Micheletto per la loro ospitalita a per avermi introdotto con Angelo Zizzola.
- La famiglia Mastrocola e Flavio per tutto quanto hanno fatto per me.
- Elena e Giuseppe per la loro immensa ospitalita.

Index